CRAVE THE ROSE: ANNE BRONTË AT 200

Nick Holland was born in Barnsley in 1971. He first encountered the Brontës when asked to read *Wuthering Heights* during his first week at University; it was the beginning of a lifelong love for the writing family who have become synonymous with his native Yorkshire.

He is now a renowned biographer, whose previous books include *In Search of Anne Brontë* (2016) and *Emily Brontë: A Life in 20 Poems* (2017), both published by The History Press, as well as *Aunt Branwell and the Brontë Legacy* (Pen & Sword, 2018). In 2016 he became the first author to complete a book signing in the Brontë Parsonage Museum in Haworth, and he has since given lectures on the Brontës nationwide.

Crave the Rose

Anne Brontë at 200

NICK HOLLAND

Valley Press

First published in 2020 by Valley Press
Woodend, The Crescent, Scarborough, YO11 2PW
www.valleypressuk.com

ISBN 978-1-912436-36-1
Cat. no. VP0156

Cover illustration by Branwell Brontë.
Cover and text design by Jamie McGarry.

Contents

Contents

'Our wishes are like tinder: the flint and steel of circumstances are continually striking out sparks, which vanish immediately, unless they chance to fall upon the tinder of our wishes; then, they instantly ignite, and the flame of hope is kindled in a moment.'

– Anne Brontë, *Agnes Grey*

Acknowledgements

L ITTLE DID I think when my first Brontë biography, *In Search of Anne Brontë*, was published in 2016 that four years later my fourth Brontë biography would be in print. I'm thrilled to be able to mark Anne Brontë's 200th anniversary in this way, and my warm and sincere thanks go to all who have made this possible.

Thanks go firstly to Jamie McGarry and all at Valley Press, especially my wonderful editor Kathryn Myers. They have shared my passion for celebrating Anne's bicentenary in print, and their dedication and support has made the process a smooth and painless one. If only Anne and Emily Brontë could have found a publisher like Jamie McGarry rather than Thomas Cautley Newby!

It's very fitting that it is this Scarborough-based publisher who has brought *Crave the Rose* into the light. Anne Brontë loved Scarborough, and has her final resting place there. I also love the resort, and I'd like to thank all those in Scarborough who have helped in the research of my book and who have always made me so welcome in the town. Particular thanks here go to Eddie Lawlor and those at St. Mary's Church.

Thanks also go to the wonderful people in Haworth and beyond who keep the Brontë flame burning, particularly to all the volunteers of the Brontë Parsonage Museum, who freely give up their time so that others may enjoy the magical home of the Brontë family.

Huge thanks go to my family and friends for their continuous support and encouragement, including Rachel

Sutcliffe, Jenny Hall, Elisabeth Basford, and many more. Equally heartfelt thanks go to all of the lovely people who have supported me on social media (you can find me on Twitter via @Nick_Holland_), you have no idea how helpful your kind words of encouragement have been, and to the many websites that continue to pay homage to the Brontës, and continue to educate and inform, especially that of Mick Armitage.

Thank you to all readers for allowing me to express my love of Anne and her family. I hope you enjoy reading this special book as much as I've enjoyed writing it, and, finally, thank you Anne Brontë – happy 200th birthday!

Preface

THE 17TH JANUARY 2020 is a special day for lovers
of literature worldwide, for it marks the 200th anniversary of the birth of Anne Brontë, the youngest of the
famous Brontë sisters.

For too long Anne has been overshadowed by her brilliant sisters Charlotte and Emily, but I believe that Anne
deserves to take a place alongside them at the very summit
of British literature. Her poetry is dazzling and heartfelt,
and her novels can seem strikingly modern, even today.
Thankfully, recent years have seen Anne Brontë, slowly
but surely, grow in recognition and renown, and 2020
is the perfect time for us all to reassess her work and acknowledge its genius in its own right.

It's for that reason that I wanted to release a new book to
mark Anne's 200th birthday. *Crave the Rose* contains three
distinct sections, creating a unifying whole which sheds
light upon the lives of Anne and her family. The first section is a brief yet revealing biography of Anne Brontë in
nine chapters. Each chapter begins with a poem by Anne,
chosen because its theme represents a moment or event in
her life that will be discussed in the chapter that follows.

Charlotte Brontë said of her sister that: 'She does not
say much for she is of a still, thoughtful nature, reserved
even with her nearest of kin.' Nevertheless Anne's voice
can be heard loud and clear in her poetry and prose,
and in her preface to the second edition of *The Tenant
of Wildfell Hall* in which she lays down her belief in the
importance of writing, and what its main purpose should

be. Through this writing, Anne's letters and diary papers, and the testimony of those who knew her and her family, we get a fulsome picture of Anne Brontë, and discover a life story that's as remarkable and tragic as any found within the covers of a Brontë novel.

The second section contains Anne's essay on faith and science, 'A Discourse Between S and C'. For many decades hidden within an archive, this is the first time this essay has ever been printed in book form. The public, wherever in the world they reside, can now read and enjoy what I believe are the final words ever written by Anne Brontë.

For this reason, this essay is of extreme importance in the Brontë story, but it also gives us a deeply personal look into Anne's life and thoughts, revealing a well-educated woman with a first class mind and a lot to say. We'll look at what the essay tells us about Anne, her beliefs and her relationships with others in Haworth Parsonage, as well as considering the evidence that could place its composition at the very end of Anne's all too brief life.

In the final section of *Crave the Rose* we have a collection of first-person encounters with the Brontës, many of which have been little known since they were included in nineteenth, and early twentieth, century newspapers and which again are now published in a book for the very first time. These are, by and large, encounters not with literary greats, the rich and famous or professional biographers, but with the ordinary people who came into contact with Anne and her family during the course of their daily lives. It allows us to see the Brontës as they really were, and the results are often revelatory and highly moving.

Let us step back in time two hundred years now, and witness a joyous event in the parsonage building of Thornton, Bradford, in the West Riding of Yorkshire.

1: Such Tears as Children Weep

'SHE'S GONE – and twice the summer's sun
   Has gilt Regina's towers,
And melted wild Angora's snows,
   And warmed Exina's bowers.
The flowerets twice on hill and dale
   Have bloomed and died away,
And twice the rustling forest leaves
   Have fallen to decay,
And thrice stern winter's icy hand
   Has checked the river's flow,
And three times o'er the mountains thrown
   His spotless robe of snow.
Two summers, springs and autumns sad
   Three winters cold and grey –
And is it then so long ago
   That wild November day!
They say such tears as children weep
   Will soon be dried away,
That childish grief however strong
   Is only for a day,
And parted friends how dear soe'er
   Will soon forgotten be;
It may be so with other hearts,
   It is not thus with me.
My mother, thou wilt weep no more
   For thou art gone above,
But can I ever cease to mourn
   Thy good and fervent love?

While that was mine the world to me
Was sunshine bright and fair;
No feeling rose within my heart
But thou couldst read it there.
And thou couldst feel for all my joys
And all my childish cares
And never weary of my play
Or scorn my foolish fears.
Beneath thy sweet maternal smile
All pain and sorrow fled,
And even the very tears were sweet
Upon thy bosom shed.
Thy loss can never be repaired;
I shall not know again
While life remains, the peaceful joy
That filled my spirit then.
Where shall I find a heart like thine
While life remains to me,
And where shall I bestow the love
I ever bore for thee?'

('An Orphan's Lament', dated 1ˢᵗ January 1841)

The 17ᵗʰ of January 1820 was one of joy for Maria Brontë and her husband Patrick, as it was on this day, in the Thornton Parsonage building they called home, that she gave birth to her fifth daughter and sixth child in total. She was given the name Anne after both Maria's elder sister and her own mother and two hundred years later she is still talked about and loved as the youngest of that legendary writing trio: the Brontë sisters.

Anne Brontë was born into a happy and prospering family, and just three months after her birth she, her four sisters and one brother, her father and mother and their two servants Nancy and Sarah Garrs, moved from Thornton to a new home in Haworth. It was a time full of promise for the Brontë family, and the happy, smiling baby seemed a portent of cloudless years to come, but it was not to be. Just a year and a half after Anne's birth her mother was dead, and it was not to be her only childhood loss. As we see from Anne's lament above, she may have been too young to comprehend the death of her mother, but she felt it deeply as the years went by and the loss burned always within her heart. This is evident not only from the poem above but from the opening page of Anne's first novel, *Agnes Grey*, in which she pays tribute to a mother she had never known except in tales passed on by her siblings, father and aunt:

'My mother, who married him against the wishes of her friends, was a squire's daughter, and a woman of spirit. In vain it was represented to her, that if she became the poor parson's wife, she must relinquish her carriage and her lady's-maid, and all the luxuries and elegancies of affluence; which to her were little less than the necessities of life. A carriage and a lady's-maid were great conveniences; but, thank Heaven, she had feet to carry her, and hands to minister to her own necessities. An elegant house and spacious grounds were not to be despised; but she would rather live in a cottage with Richard Grey than in a palace with any man in the world.'[1]

For Richard Grey we can read Anne's father the poor parson, Patrick Brontë, who was indeed living in a cottage at the time of his wedding to Maria, the inauspiciously named Lousy Thorn Cottage in Hartshead, where he was then parish priest. In the portrait of Alice Grey we also see a clear representation of Anne's mother, or at least of the impression that Anne had gained of her from her relatives, and whilst she may not have been the daughter of a 'country squire' she was indeed from a grand background.

Maria Branwell, as she was called before her marriage to Patrick, was the eleventh and penultimate child of Thomas Branwell and Anne Carne, and she was born in 1783 into one of the leading families in Penzance society and commerce. The Cornish town of Penzance was thriving in the late eighteenth century, and her father's fortunes were on the rise. An indication of this can be seen in the will he wrote in the final weeks of his life in 1808 in which he listed properties across Penzance and beyond, including the town's only mansion, an inn, a brewery, shops and his own warehouse on Penzance quay.[2]

Thomas was also an alderman on the town's council, but in 1809 Maria's elder brother Benjamin went one step further by becoming Mayor of Penzance. It was a comfortable life on the Cornish coast for Maria, with warm, sun-filled summers, a women's library accessible to wealthier families such as the Branwells, and Assembly Rooms modelled on those made famous in Bath by Jane Austen, filled with music, dancing and, on the still, warm nights of summer, a tantalising promise of romance. The deaths within a year of each other of her father and mother, however, in 1808 and 1809 forced her to reassess her situation.

At first, it seems that Maria continued to live in Chapel Street, Penzance with two sisters that she had grown close to, her elder sister Elizabeth and younger sister Charlotte, but just as Anne said of Alice Grey in her début novel, Maria Branwell was a woman of spirit and determined to make her own way in life rather than living on her annuity.

It was for this reason that in 1812 Maria responded to an invitation from her father's sister, her Aunt Jane Fennell, to work at a Methodist school known as Woodhouse Grove which she and her husband, John, had recently opened in Apperley Bridge. Her decision to take the job was no light undertaking, as Apperley Bridge was in the West Riding of Yorkshire, over four hundred miles from her Cornish home. In those days such a journey was an arduous, sometimes dangerous one, and travellers would often write their will before commencing such a voyage.

The danger inherent in the journey was shown in a letter by Maria lamenting the news that the ship containing her possessions, presumably sent on after her by her older sister Elizabeth, had been shipwrecked and the vast majority of her possessions destroyed[3]. Thankfully, Maria Branwell arrived safely in Apperley Bridge in the summer of 1812, as did another person a long way from home: Patrick Brontë.

Patrick came from a very different background to Maria. Not for him a life of comfort in a large home, not for him dancing, music and leisure. He was the son of a poor farming family in County Down, in what is now Northern Ireland, but a twist of fate changed his life, Maria's life and literary history forever.

As a child he attended weaving classes, and one day he was sitting outside the weaver's house reading aloud from *Paradise Lost* by John Milton. By happy chance, passing by at that very moment was the local Anglican priest Thomas Tighe, who was immediately struck by the excellence of this poor child's reading. From that moment on Tighe, a man of independent wealth and philanthropic spirit, took a keen interest in Patrick's education and life. He allowed Patrick to attend a school he ran, and whilst still in his teens Patrick progressed to teaching there, before eventually opening his own school as well as acting as a tutor to Tighe's own children.[4] This was obviously a young man of prodigious talents, talents which would be lost if he was to have a career tilling the field or weaving. With this in mind, Tighe arranged for Patrick to attend his old college, St. John's at Cambridge University, leading to a career as a minister in the Church of England. It was a very different life to the one the young boy in County Down could have envisaged, but it was one he carried out with fidelity and brilliance for the rest of his days.

Maria of Cornwall and Patrick of Ireland arrived at Woodhouse Grove school in Yorkshire at around the same time in the summer of 1812. She was then in her late 20s and he in his mid-30s, two people hundreds of miles from the homes and families they had known, no longer in the first flush of youth, but ready to make their way in life, whatever it should bring. It brought them each other, and they fell quickly in love, marrying at St. Oswald's church, Guiseley, on 12th December, less than half a year after they had first met. It was an unusual ceremony in many ways, for marrying at the same ceremony was Maria's cousin Jane Fennell who also worked at Woodhouse Grove school and Reverend William Morgan, a Welsh priest who was an old friend of Patrick's from earlier ministries in Shropshire. The two ministers performed the ceremonies for each other, with the two brides also acting as bridesmaids. Morgan remained a lifelong friend of Patrick and it was he who baptised Anne Brontë in 1820; it was he who also later had to perform the funeral services of many of the children he had baptised.

To add to the unique circumstances of this wedding, by prior arrangement between the three parties, Maria Branwell's younger sister Charlotte, also a cousin of Jane Fennell of course, married yet another cousin, Joseph

Branwell, at the exact same time over four hundred miles away in Penzance. As Charlotte Branwell's daughter later recalled with touching understatement:

'It is but seldom that two sisters and four cousins are united in holy matrimony on the same day.'[5]

Patrick and Maria's marriage was a happy and productive one, and by early 1815 they had two daughters, Maria named after her mother and Elizabeth after her Cornish aunt; with a growing family, the Brontës needed a larger home and this was the driving force behind Patrick's move to the parish of Thornton, which crucially came with its own grace and favour parsonage, shortly after Elizabeth Brontë's birth.

Soon however, even Thornton's Parsonage was becoming crowded, as the years from 1816 to 1818 saw three more additions to the family in quick succession: Charlotte, Patrick Branwell who would become forever known by his middle name, and Emily Jane. By this time, Patrick was writing to his Bishop and friends to complain that Thornton Parsonage was ill-constructed and inconvenient for a family of his size[6]. By May 1819 it seemed that his prayers had been answered as he was offered the curacy of Haworth, a moorside parish around five miles from Thornton, which came with a larger parsonage building and more than a little prestige as it had formerly been the parish of the celebrated Methodist preacher, William Grimshaw.

By the following month, however, complications had arisen, as reported by the Leeds Intelligencer:

'We hear that the Rev. P. Brontë, curate of Thornton, has been nominated by the vicar of Bradford, to the valuable perpetual curacy of Haworth, vacated by the death of the Rev. James Charnock; but that the inhabitants of the chapelry intend to resist the presentation, and have entered a caveat accordingly.'[7]

The parish elders of Haworth had a long-standing and, as far as they were concerned, legally-sound tradition of nominating their own priest to the vicar of Bradford whose decision it was in theory. Patrick became aware of the villagers' objections, purely on the grounds that he had been selected by Bradford's vicar Henry Heap without any consultation, and stepped aside. The succeeding months in Haworth descended into a dark and dangerous farce; Heap once again tried to impose his own choice of priest on Haworth, this time in the shape of Samuel Redhead, and many years later the Bishop of Ripon, Charles Longley, recalled the extreme and violent measures the villagers took against him:

'There is an ancient feud between Bradford and Haworth… the people of Haworth can by the trust deed of the living, prevent the person appointed by the vicar [of Bradford] from entering the Parsonage or receiving any of the emoluments, if he does not please them… in the case of Mr Redhead, the inhabitants exercised their right of resistance and opposition and to such a point did they carry it, that they actually brought a Donkey into the church while Mr Redhead was officiating and held up its head to stare him in the face – they then laid a plan to crush him to death in the vestry, by pushing a table against him as he was taking off his surplice and hanging it up, foiled in this for some reason or other they then turned out into the Churchyard where Mr Redhead was going to perform a funeral and were determined to throw him into the grave and bury him alive.'[8]

Redhead could not return to his duties, and after negotiations between Bradford's vicar and Haworth's parishioners, a compromise was reached – one that finally saw Patrick Brontë move to Haworth on 20th April 1820 to take up a position he would hold for more than forty years. On that spring morning he walked at the head of the seven carts carrying his belongings and family up the steep and cobbled Kirkgate and onto Parsonage Lane (now known to tourists from across the globe as Haworth's Main Street and Church Lane). In one of the carts his wife, Maria, nursed their three-month-old daughter; this would be the home that Anne Brontë would know and love, but unbeknownst to all, her mother was entering the last months of her life.

On 29th January 1821, just 12 days after Anne's first birthday, Maria Brontë was gripped by a terrible pain that grew worse over the weeks and months ahead. A despairing Patrick sought all the medical assistance he could, almost bankrupting himself in the process, but his wife's condition continued to deteriorate. The six Brontë children were too young to comprehend the enormity of what was happening, but the atmosphere of pain and anguish must have been keenly felt by all but the toddling Anne. It is said that Maria, on her protracted deathbed, would only see one of her children at a time, as seeing them together, knowing that she was about to leave them, was more than she could bear.

After eight terrible months, Maria's struggle was over, although Anne's orphan lament was only beginning. Many years later Charlotte Brontë was given some of the sweet letters written from her mother to her father during their courtship, and after paying tribute to the fine mind exhibited within them she was left to mourn, 'I wish she had lived, and that I had known her.'9 Charlotte was five years old when her mother passed away so retained some memories of her, but Anne would have had none, and yet it seems that in many ways Anne is the sibling who most mirrored her mother's traits.

Maria was a devoutly Christian woman, as was her youngest child and, like Anne, she also believed that suffering in this world can prepare us for a better life to come. Evidence of this is found throughout Maria's long essay, 'The Advantages of Poverty in Religious Concerns', and one section is particularly touching in light of her fate:

'Is it not an evil to be deprived of the necessaries of life? Can there be any anguish equal to that occasioned by objects, dear as your own soul, famishing with cold and hunger? Is it not an evil to hear the heart-rending cries of your children craving for that which you have it not in your power to give them? And, as an aggravation of this distress, to know that some are surfeited by abundance at the same time that you and yours are perishing for want?'[10]

Maria's answer to this conundrum within her essay is that yes, this is an evil, but it is outweighed by the bliss that a heavenly afterlife can bring, a view shared by Anne and often alluded to in her writing. Throughout her life Anne heard stories of her mother, until she became an almost mythological embodiment of goodness, as exemplified in her poem above. Perhaps at the back of Anne's mind too there was a nagging question of whether she had been in some way responsible for her mother's death. Whilst it is frequently said that Maria died of uterine cancer, a prominent twentieth century obstetrician opined that this was unlikely given the known circumstances, and that the most likely diagnosis was chronic pelvic sepsis and anaemia, a condition that would have been developing from the moment Maria gave birth to her final child, Anne.[11]

As we shall see, Anne's Aunt Elizabeth came to take on a maternal role in Anne's life, but as an infant she would also have looked up to her oldest sisters Maria and Elizabeth. They were ever ready with the love and support Anne needed. Patrick described his second daughter Elizabeth as having 'good solid sense',[12] whilst he was abundant in praise for the prodigious talents shown by his eldest daughter Maria, saying that he could converse with her upon any leading topics of the day with as much pleasure as if he were discussing them with an adult.[13]

The Brontë children were largely taught at home, but Patrick, drawing upon the life-changing effect it had brought him, was a firm believer in the power of formal education, so in the summer of 1823 Maria and Elizabeth were sent for a term at the highly-regarded Crofton Hall school near Wakefield. This school had once been attended by two women known to Patrick from Thornton: Elizabeth Firth and Fanny Outhwaite. They were Anne's godparents and it is likely that they recommended the school to Patrick and probably helped with the fees too.

It became clear, however, that this excellent school was just too expensive for the Brontë children, especially if Patrick hoped to send his three younger daughters there after Maria and Elizabeth. He looked around for another suitable establishment that would be more within his means, and by the summer of the following year he believed he had found just the place.

The Clergy Daughter's School was in the secluded location of Cowan Bridge, in what was then Westmorland and is now in Lancashire at the foot of the Lake District. As the name suggests, it was exclusively for daughters of the Anglican clergy, and it had subsidised fees of fourteen pounds per year. Maria and Elizabeth were sent to Cowan

Bridge on 21st July 1824; Charlotte, whose journey had been delayed by illness, followed on 10th August, and Emily, aged six at the time, arrived in Cowan Bridge on 25th November of that year. It was a terrible mistake.

Cowan Bridge was far removed from what Crofton Hall had been, from what any school should be. Food was meagre and unwholesome, discipline was rigidly enforced by its Calvinist founder William Carus Wilson, and the whole aspect of the school was cold and unhealthy. The stern Wilson has now been immortalised as Mr Brocklehurst in *Jane Eyre* and the school is portrayed viscerally as Lowood. In later years, Wilson threatened to sue Elizabeth Gaskell for repeating Charlotte's assertion of what the school had been like, and after Charlotte's death he also became embroiled in a heated argument with Haworth curate Arthur Bell Nicholls, by then Charlotte's widow, via a series of letters printed in newspapers. Nevertheless, Charlotte insisted that Cowan Bridge was, if anything, worse than she had portrayed it in her brilliant novel, and whoever has read *Jane Eyre* will surely recall her description of this sepulchral school:

'That forest-dell, where Lowood lay, was the cradle of fog and fog-bred pestilence; which, quickening with the quickening spring, crept into the Orphan Asylum, breathed typhus through its crowded schoolroom and dormitory, and, ere May arrived, transformed the seminary into a hospital.'[14]

Reality followed the path of Charlotte's fiction and by May 1825 an outbreak of tuberculosis (then known as consumption) within the close quarters of Cowan Bridge had left many of the pupils ill and dying. Among them were Maria Brontë, so beloved of her sisters, the girl as bright as any adult, and who had placed a protective arm around her younger siblings, and Elizabeth Brontë, practical, stoic, kind and loving. After being sent back to Haworth mortally ill, Maria died aged eleven on 6th May and Elizabeth died aged ten on 15th June 1825. They were the first Brontë siblings to die of tuberculosis, but they were far from the last.

Anne Brontë was now five years old, and she had already lost her mother and her two eldest sisters. The deeply sensitive child became a deeply sensitive woman; she would never forget their names, would never stop thinking of what they could have been, and how different her life would have been with them around her. The six Brontë children were now four, but through adversity they became an increasingly tight-knit unit. Let the outside world bring what it may, the four Brontë siblings always had each other, and that solidarity would soon find expression in a collective obsession with writing.

2: A Young Enthusiast

'THAT WIND IS from the North, I know it well;
　No other breeze could have so wild a swell.
Now deep and loud it thunders round my cell,
Then faintly dies,
And softly sighs,
And moans and murmurs mournfully.
I know its language; thus it speaks to me –
"I have passed over thy own mountains dear,
Thy northern mountains – and they still are free,
Still lonely, wild, majestic, bleak and drear,
And stern and lovely, as they used to be
When thou, a young enthusiast,
As wild and free as they,
O'er rocks and glens and snowy heights
Didst often love to stray.
I've blown the wild untrodden snows
In whirling eddies from their brows,
And I have howled in caverns wild
Where thou, a joyous mountain child,
Didst dearly love to be.
The sweet world is not changed, but thou
Art pining in a dungeon now,
Where thou must ever be;
No voice but mine can reach thine ear,
And Heaven has kindly sent me here,
To mourn and sigh with thee,
And tell thee of the cherished land
Of thy nativity."

Blow on, wild wind, thy solemn voice,
However sad and drear,
Is nothing to the gloomy silence
I have had to bear.
Hot tears are streaming from my eyes,
But these are better far
Than that dull gnawing tearless time
The stupor of despair.
Confined and hopeless as I am,
O speak of liberty,
O tell me of my mountain home,
And I will welcome thee.'

('The North Wind', dated 26th January 1838)

Anne Brontë would never know her mother other than from the stories told by others, and perhaps the greatest source of these stories was the woman who came to replace her in Anne's life: her Aunt Elizabeth, more commonly known as Aunt Branwell.

Elizabeth Branwell was seven years the senior of her sister Maria, but she never married, and instead forged close bonds with her younger sisters, Maria and Charlotte and with her elder sister Jane, who as we shall see later had a significant influence upon Anne's masterpiece *The Tenant of Wildfell Hall*.

The closeness between Elizabeth and Maria in particular is shown by the fact that in 1815, despite the daunting nature of the journey involved, Elizabeth Branwell travelled from Penzance to Thornton in order to be able to serve as godmother at the baptism of the niece who was named after her. She remained in Thornton for over a year, meaning that she was present for the birth of her niece, Charlotte, as well. During her time in Thornton she cultivated a friendship with Elizabeth Firth of Kipping Hall in the village and also struck up a friendship with her brother-in-law, Patrick Brontë. Four months before Elizabeth finally left Thornton in the summer of 1816 she was presented with a personal gift from him – a book of his own poems entitled *The Rural Minstrel*,[1] complete with a personal tribute to his sister-in-law:

'Gift of the author to his beloved sister Miss Branwell as a small token of affection and esteem. Thornton nr Bradford. March 29 1816'[2]

It is easy to imagine Elizabeth Branwell taking a last look over her shoulder as she left Yorkshire on her return journey to Cornwall, her heart filled with sadness at the thought that in all probability she would never see Elizabeth Firth, Patrick Brontë, her three nieces or her dear sister Maria again. This was the reason for her extended stay, it was not the kind of journey that could be repeated again and again. In very different circumstances, however, Elizabeth found herself travelling back from Cornwall to Yorkshire just five years later.

A letter from Patrick had informed Elizabeth of the perilous state her sister was in and, in an action typical of her, Elizabeth set out immediately so that she could nurse Maria in her final days and weeks. One of her first acts after arriving in Haworth in the summer of 1821 was to dismiss the woman who had been hired to nurse Maria, after which she took over the duties herself. It was this woman, Martha Wright, who was the source of the unjustified comments against Patrick and Aunt Branwell that found their way into Elizabeth Gaskell's biography of Charlotte Brontë,[3] but it was also she who gave us the earliest description of the Brontë children, including the infant Anne:

'But there never were such good children... they were good little creatures.'[4]

After Maria finally passed from this world just a few months after Elizabeth's arrival, she could, after a suitable period of mourning, have returned to Penzance where her sisters Jane and Charlotte awaited her, but something made her stay. Doubtless she remembered Maria's fears of what would happen to her children after her death and, equally doubtless, something moved within Elizabeth's heart when she looked upon the six motherless children. Elizabeth Gaskell portrayed her Branwell namesake as a very formal, almost unfeeling, woman, but when we look deeper we see that this is far removed from the truth. Elizabeth Branwell always placed family concerns above her own, and there is no better indication of her innate sense of duty than the fact that she never saw the sunny skies above Penzance again. She looked at Maria, Elizabeth, Charlotte, Branwell, Emily and, especially, Anne, and knew that this was where her heart was. The delights of Cornwall meant nothing to her compared to these six children. She would stay in cold, moorland Haworth until the day she died. Elizabeth Branwell became Aunt Branwell, and, more than that, she became a second mother to the children who needed love, support and direction.

This was a great comfort to Patrick as well, of course, as he confided to his friend John Buckland:

'Her sister, Miss Branwell, arrived, and afforded great comfort to my mind, which has been the case ever since, by sharing my labours and sorrows, and behaving as an affectionate mother to my children.'[5]

Her guiding hand was needed even more after the deaths of her nieces, Maria and Elizabeth, and by that time she had become indispensable particularly to Anne, just as Anne had become to her. Anne was one year old when Aunt Branwell moved into Haworth Parsonage, and it is natural that her heart was captured by the helpless infant, who had so recently been nursed by her beloved sister. Anne's cot was placed into her aunt's room, and they continued to share a room throughout Anne's childhood. Elizabeth Branwell's was the face Anne saw every night and morning throughout her formative years, hers the kiss placed on Anne's forehead before the candle was blown out, hers the advice she always sought, and a strong and loving bond grew between the aunt and niece as much as between any mother and daughter.

The influence of Elizabeth Branwell's caring nature and her strong faith can be seen in Anne in later life, as can her emphasis on the value of spiritual treasures rather than material goods. The bond between them was evident to all who saw it, as we can see from Ellen Nussey's report after visiting the Parsonage for the first of many times in summer 1833:

'Anne, dear, gentle Anne, was quite different in appearance from the others. She was her aunt's favourite. Her hair was a very pretty, light brown, and fell on her neck in graceful curls. She had lovely violet-blue eyes, fine pencilled eyebrows, and clear, almost transparent complexion.'[6]

This is the first description we have of Anne Brontë, at the time aged thirteen, and as later descriptions do it emphasises the fact that she looked markedly different to her siblings. It is also often said that Anne was the prettiest of the Brontës, and there seems to be a similarity between pictures of Anne drawn by Charlotte and a picture of her mother Maria drawn in Penzance in 1799 by James Tonkin[7]. Could another reason why Anne's aunt loved her especially be that she was the one Brontë sibling who carried the Branwell looks?

Ellen Nussey was the great friend of Charlotte Brontë, and we shall see how she came to play a crucial role in Anne's life too. Her report of this first encounter with the Brontës in Haworth also reveals the other close familial bond in Anne's life – that with her sister Emily. The two youngest Brontës formed a connection that Ellen described as twin-like and without interruption, and she gave a moving description of this sibling symbiosis in a letter to Elizabeth Gaskell:

'She [Emily] and gentle Anne were often seen twined together as united statues of power and humility – they were to be seen with their arms lacing each other in their younger days whenever their occupation permitted their union.'[8]

There was a year and a half difference in age between Emily and Anne, but that was enough for the elder sister to take the leading role in their relationship, and Anne grew up copying what Emily did, and learning from her actions and opinions. One example of this is that Anne shared with Emily a love of nature and the outdoors, and the natural world at its most powerful would forever be thrilling to them. They saw just that on 2nd September 1824. On that day the Garrs sisters led Emily, Branwell and four-year-old Anne Brontë on a walk across the moors (the three older sisters all being in attendance at Cowan Bridge school at the time). A spell of stormy weather had left Emily especially raring to get outside again and, where she led, Anne was sure to follow. Unfortunately, the inclement weather also brought about a freak event that could have ended the Brontë story before it had begun.

As they walked the moors, dark clouds gathered overhead, heavy rain fell, the earth shook and a rumbling noise grew in intensity. Nancy and Sarah Garrs knew that something was badly wrong and hearing a voice calling to them from a nearby house, they ran for cover and found it just in time to avoid a huge torrent of mud, water and rock that spread across the moors like a land tsunami. It has come to be known as the Crow Hill Bog Burst, a vast explosion of water and matter caused by a landslip, and the scars can still be seen across the moorland landscape today. Huge rocks were thrown in the air, and streams and brooks were filled with dead fish for weeks afterwards. A local newspaper reported on the brush with death that the Brontë children had endured:

'Somebody gave alarm, and thereby saved the lives of some children who would otherwise have been swept away.'[9]

The place where they found sanctuary was the porch of Ponden Hall, a place which became a regular destination for Anne's and Emily's walks in later years, and its box bed with shuttered window has become immortalised in *Wuthering Heights*. On one hand this was clearly a terrifying ordeal, for the children themselves, and for their father and aunt looking fearfully out of the Parsonage window, but on the other hand it also enthralled the young minds of Emily and Anne. It began a lifelong love of extreme weather, and whilst the rugged moorlands would always be Emily's favourite terrain, Anne would later prefer the foaming waves of the sea crashing upon the rocks of Yorkshire's coastline.

Another trait that united Emily and Anne was their extreme shyness, and it is said that they sometimes hid from unexpected visitors to their parsonage home, taking refuge behind doors and beneath tables. Elizabeth Gaskell, however, made a distinction between the two sisters in this matter:

'Emily was a tall, long-armed girl, more fully grown than her elder sister; extremely reserved in manner. I distinguish reserve from shyness, because I imagine shyness would please, if it knew how; whereas, reserve is indifferent whether it pleases or not. Anne, like her eldest sister [Charlotte], was shy; Emily was reserved.'[10]

This may be harsh on Emily, especially as Elizabeth Gaskell met neither her nor Anne, but it is true to say that whilst Emily retreated further into her inner world in adult life, Anne fought and conquered her shyness, holding down jobs for far longer than any of her siblings.

Shyness was endemic among all four Brontë children, especially after the deaths of their two eldest sisters. They became a close-knit family unit, shutting out the eternal world which had brought danger and death. At the head of this four-strong company was Charlotte, now the oldest sibling, and one activity more than any other delighted them: writing.

There are a number of ingredients that helped to shape the Brontës as writers. Their father had an extremely enlightened attitude to education, especially the education of women. He allowed his daughters free access to his magazines and his library, whereas many fathers of this time would have banned their daughters from seeing works by the likes of Byron and Shelley. Aunt Branwell must also take some credit here, for despite her reputation for austerity and a supposed compulsion for forcing her nieces to sew for hour upon hour, she too was a lover of books and must have agreed with Patrick's decision to let the girls read and learn.

We know that Aunt Branwell herself subscribed to magazines that included literary extracts and reviews, and that she let her nieces read them too. At Christmas

1828 she bought them a new book by Walter Scott entitled *Tales of a Grandfather*. It was an exciting retelling of Scotland's history tailored for the younger reader, and it helped to spark in the Brontës a love of all things Scottish, and particularly for the works of Scott himself. Six years after this thoughtful gift, Charlotte Brontë wrote to a friend: 'For Fiction – read Scott alone, all novels after his are worthless.'[11]

An even more influential gift arrived at the parsonage on 5th June 1826 in the shape of a dozen wooden soldiers. Patrick had returned from Leeds with presents for all his children, including a dancing doll for young Anne. The soldiers were ostensibly a gift for Branwell, but the four close-knit siblings soon shared them out. A young Charlotte wrote of how she snatched up her favourite and named it after her hero, the Duke of Wellington, whereas the mischievous Branwell decided that his favourite would be Wellington's nemesis, Napoleon Bonaparte. Emily and Anne chose Arctic explorers, Ross and Parry, to be personified by their soldiers, but Charlotte also revealed:

'When Anne came down, she said one should be hers. Mine was the prettiest of the whole, and the tallest, and the most perfect in every part. Emily's was a grave-looking fellow, and we called him 'Gravey'. Anne's was a queer little thing, much like herself, and we called him 'Waiting-boy'.[12]

Charlotte was nearly thirteen at the time she wrote this, and increasingly conscious of her diminutive stature, so we can forgive her the slightly dismissive comments that are so typical of siblings that age talking of younger siblings then and now. It does remind us of another portrait of the young Anne Brontë however, this time from her father Patrick. Realising how shy his children were he hit upon the notion of placing each child in turn behind a mask, and asking them a question that they would then be able to answer free from their usual reserve:

'I began with the youngest (Anne, afterwards Acton Bell) and asked what a child like her most wanted; she answered, "Age and experience".'[13] This then seems to be a common denominator in Anne's childhood, she was wanting and waiting, but the world would not have to wait long to find out what she was waiting for.

Charlotte took the lead in choosing a toy soldier, and she also took the lead in orchestrating the games that developed around them. At first these took the form of improvised play sessions, but soon the book-loving Brontës started putting the adventures of 'the twelve', also known as 'the young men' down on paper. As the oldest siblings Charlotte and Branwell took the lead in this venture, inventing a land of intrigue for the soldiers and the characters that developed from them. At first this land was called the Glass Town Confederacy, with the great glass town of Verdopolis at its centre, but as their ambitions grew so did this imaginary land, into the kingdom of Angria.

It is Angria that hosts the incredible little books that Charlotte and Branwell wrote. It was a prodigious output, written down in tiny books in minuscule writing, which is so small we need a strong microscope to read it today. These books are incredibly detailed, from the hand-stitched covers to the satirical adverts mocking those found within magazines such as Blackwell's that the young Brontës devoured. This Angrian juvenilia is often brilliantly written, amusing and intriguing by turns, but although Anne and Emily sometimes appear as characters within the tales under the guises of Chief Genius Annii and Chief Genius Emmii, or as the characters of Ross and Parry, they are written exclusively by Charlotte and Branwell.

Things changed dramatically when Charlotte left for a new school in January 1831. Patrick and Aunt Branwell had been schooling the sisters themselves since the Cowan Bridge tragedies, but they knew that a formal education of some kind was important if the girls were to grow up to become governesses or teachers, the most likely professions awaiting them. Eventually Patrick found a new school, Roe Head in Mirfield, and one of the things that may have appealed to him is that his old friend from Thornton, Anne's godmother Elizabeth Firth, now Mrs Franks, was living nearby and would be able to keep a protective eye on his children.

Thankfully it was a good choice; Roe Head was very different to Cowan Bridge, with a caring, nurturing environment at its heart, thanks to its kindly headmistress, Miss Margaret Wooler. Charlotte spent a year and a half as a pupil at Roe Head and it was there that she met her two great, lifelong friends, Ellen Nussey and Mary Taylor, but it also brought the Brontë quartet and their Angrian 'scribblemania', as Charlotte called it, to a sudden halt.

With their oldest sister absent, Anne and Emily were thrown, to their delight, even closer together, and they soon recognised the opportunity this gave them to venture into writing themselves. Leaving the Angria of Charlotte and Branwell aside, they created their own imaginary land of Gondal. Unlike the desert-like Angria, Gondal was an island in the Pacific Ocean, although it had mountainous, moorland landscapes that seemed more redolent of the Pennine landscape they knew and loved than a tropical paradise.

Unfortunately the Gondal prose created by Anne and

Emily is lost to posterity, but we know it must have been a vast collection as they often refer to it in their diary papers. Anne and Emily had formed a habit of writing diary papers recording a snapshot of a particular day, which they would then seal and read again years later when they came to write the next paper. We currently have diary papers written in the years 1834, 1837, 1841 and 1845, although there may have been others that are now lost. The first two were written jointly by Anne and Emily (complete with charming sketches by Emily) but the papers of 1841 and 1845 were composed separately by the two sisters, revealing the change which had taken place in Anne's life by that time.

The very first diary paper gives a revealing glimpse of the teenage sisters; they are not austere and serious, they are playful and have much in common with any teenager of today:

'Anne and I have been peeling apples for Charlotte to make an apple pudding... Tabby said just now come Anne pilloputate (ie pill a potato) Aunt has come into the kitchen just now and said 'where are your feet Anne?' Anne answered 'On the floor Aunt'... The Gondals are discovering the interior of Gaaldine, Sally Mosley is washing in the back kitchin. It is past Twelve o'clock Anne and I have not tided ourselves, done our bed work done our lessons and we want to go out to play. We are going to have for dinner boiled beef, turnips, potato's and apple pudding, the kitchin is in a very untidy state. Anne and I have not done our music exercise which consists of b major... Anne and I say I wonder what we shall be like and what we shall be and where we shall be if all goes on well in the year 1874 – in which year I shall be in my 57th year, Anne will be going in her 55th year, Branwell will be going in his 58th year and Charlotte in her 59th year, hoping we shall all be well at that time we close our paper, Emily and Anne.'[14]

The ending of this diary paper is profoundly touching in light of what was to come, but the paper as a whole is barely punctuated and strewn with spelling errors. We get a much better indication of the early power of Anne Brontë's writing from the poems that she began to compose around this time. The Gondal prose is lost, but thankfully we still have examples of the verse that Anne and Emily composed about this kingdom, and the poem at the head of this chapter, written by an eighteen-year-old Anne, is the fifth earliest that still exists. The very first of Anne's poems still known to exist dates from December 1836, and is entitled 'Verses by Lady Geralda'. It begins:

'Why, when I hear the stormy breath
Of the wild winter wind
Rushing o'er the mountain heath,
Does sadness fill my mind?
For long ago I loved to lie
Upon the pathless moor,
To hear the wild wind rushing by
With never ceasing roar;
Its sound was music then to me;
Its wild and lofty voice
Made my heart beat exultingly
And my whole soul rejoice.
But now, how different is the sound?
It takes another tone,
And howls along the barren ground
With melancholy moan.'[15]

These, then, are the first written words of Anne Brontë that we have, and they are a perfect introduction to the Gondal poetry, which she composed alongside Emily. Lady Geralda only appears in this one poem, although she may be the same character as Emily's heroine, Geraldine. The melancholy tone is so typical of the Gondal work produced by the youngest Brontës; it is a land far removed from the often humorous Angria of Charlotte and Branwell, for this land is one of high passions, low treachery, intrigue, lust and despair. The natural landscape, so reminiscent of Haworth, is also a continual feature in the poetry that was subsequently to come from both Anne and Emily.

Masks of one kind or another feature often in Anne's story. We find her as a child behind the physical mask her father placed upon her. In later years she adopted the mask of Acton Bell to publish her novels, and her Gondal verse is also frequently a mask: one which allowed her to express her true feelings, her hopes and fears, by setting it in a faraway land and expressing it through the voice of others.

Anne's earliest extant poem is also one of her longest, and she herself records that it is exactly one hundred lines long at the end of her manuscript. Within these lines we hear Geralda's tale of her tragic family, but we also hear Anne's concerns for a matter that was very pressing for her in December 1836. She no longer loves to lie on the pathless moor (as she and Emily had done so often in the real world), and the whistling wind no longer cheers her. The poem concludes with these words:

> 'I leave thee then, my childhood's home,
> For all thy joys are gone;

I leave thee through the world to roam
In search of fair renown,
From such a hopeless home to part
Is happiness to me,
For nought can charm my weary heart
Except activity.'[16]

Here we have a direct glimpse into Anne's life at the time she put her quill to paper to write these words. Anne had indeed left her childhood home by this time, and her heart was weary when she thought of the moors she loved and could no longer see, for in the autumn of 1835 Anne Brontë had embarked upon a journey that shaped the woman she was to become. For the first time, at the age of fifteen, she was sent to school. It was an experience that changed her life, and one that almost ended it.

3: A Wretch's Prayer

'I HAVE GONE backward in the work,
  The labour has not sped,
Drowsy and dark my spirit lies,
Heavy and dull as lead.
How can I rouse my sinking soul
From such a lethargy?
How can I break these iron chains,
And set my spirit free?
There have been times when I have mourned,
In anguish o'er the past;
And raised my suppliant hands on high,
While tears fell thick and fast,
And prayed to have my sins forgiven
With such a fervent zeal,
An earnest grief – a strong desire
That now I cannot feel!
And vowed to trample on my sins,
And called on Heaven to aid
My spirit in her firm resolves
And hear the vows I made.
And I have felt so full of love,
So strong in spirit then,
As if my heart would never cool
Or wander back again.
And yet, alas! how many times
My feet have gone astray,
How oft have I forgot my God,
How greatly fallen away!

My sins increase, my love grows cold,
And Hope within me dies,
And Faith itself is wavering now,
O how shall I arise!
I cannot weep but I can pray,
Then let me not despair;
Lord Jesus, save me lest I die,
And hear a wretch's prayer.'

('Despondency', dated 20th December 1841)

When Charlotte Brontë returned from her Roe Head school days in June 1832, after a year and a half as a pupil, it was intended that she would pass on all she had learnt to her younger sisters, Emily and Anne. There were no signs of the younger Brontës following Charlotte's path to Mirfield, and the reason for this must have been financial. Patrick, unlike many clergymen of his day, had no independent means of his own, and was reliant upon a wage that was eaten into by the cost of maintaining his parsonage and church property. We know that on occasion godparents provided a helping hand, and that Aunt Branwell, who was still receiving an annuity from her father's will, also helped out by insisting that she pay rent for her room at the Parsonage,[1] thus allowing her to help the Brontës without the possibility of causing offence by offering it as charity.

The catalyst for Emily and Anne to commence their own schooling, however, came in the summer of 1835, by way of an offer of employment made to Charlotte Brontë. Charlotte had obviously excelled during her months at Roe Head, and caught the attention of headmistress, Margaret Wooler, for on 29th July of that year, three years after leaving the school as a pupil, she returned as Roe Head's new teacher.

Miss Wooler's proposition was especially attractive to Charlotte as not only did it open up a teaching career for her, something she would probably have expected to do for the rest of her working life at that time, it also stated that Charlotte could bring one of her sisters with her to receive an education free of the usual fees. Not only would the two sisters have their companionship to alleviate any feelings of homesickness, it would also help to ease the financial burden on their father by leaving him with two less mouths to feed. This can be seen in a letter from Charlotte to Ellen dated 6th July 1835, but unfortunately, things did not go quite as smoothly as Charlotte envisaged:

'Yes, I am going to teach in the very school where I myself was taught. Miss Wooler made me the offer, and I preferred it to one or two proposals of private governess-ship, which I had before received. I am sad – very sad – at the thought of leaving home; but duty – necessity – these are stern mistresses, who will not be disobeyed... Emily and I leave home on the 29th of this month; the idea of being together consoles us somewhat.'[2]

Emily, as the next eldest daughter, was the obvious choice to accompany Charlotte to Roe Head, but even in the kindly atmosphere of this school she withered. In the few weeks she stayed, Emily retreated further and further into her shell, talking little and eating less, to the extent that Charlotte feared for her sister's life. No doubt she had recollections of watching Maria and Elizabeth decline at school still seared in her memory, and the trauma of seeing Emily fade in similar fashion was still vivid in 1850, when Charlotte wrote of it:

'She found in the bleak solitude [of Haworth] many

and dear delights; and not the least and best loved – was liberty. Liberty was the breath of Emily's nostrils; without it, she perished. The change from her own home to a school, and from her own very noiseless, very secluded, but unrestricted and inartificial mode of life, to one of disciplined routine (though under the kindliest auspices) was what she failed in enduring. Her nature proved here too strong for her fortitude. Every morning when she woke, the vision of home and the moors rushed on her, and darkened and saddened the day that lay before her. Nobody knew what ailed her but me – I knew only too well. In this struggle her health was quickly broken; her white face, attenuated form, and failing strength threatened rapid decline. I felt in my heart she would die, if she did not go home.'[3]

After Charlotte expressed these fears in a letter home, Patrick wasted no time in recalling Emily to Haworth, but he must also have been convinced that on this occasion no fault could be found in the school itself, for by October 1835 he had sent his youngest daughter, Anne, in her place. This was to be Anne's first taste of formal education, and yet she was far from uneducated. She had studied hard with her father and aunt, and when alone or with her brother and sisters, and had already shown an aptitude and passion for learning. She was particularly keen on studying the Bible, and she became the only Brontë daughter who could read and speak Latin. Not only had Anne been reading and learning voraciously in her pre-school years, she was also acting as a teacher herself as her father employed her talents in the Sunday school he had had built adjacent to the Parsonage.

Serving as a teacher in the Sunday school provided good practice for her likely future career, but it must have been a testing ordeal for the shy teenage girl with a quiet voice. We see a reflection of her first experiences as a teacher in her sister Charlotte's novel *Shirley*. The heroine Caroline Helstone is largely modelled on Anne, just as the titular character Shirley Keeldar is a portrait of Emily, and so the portrayal of Caroline as a teacher is surely based upon Charlotte's memory of her youngest sister in the same situation:

'They made her a Sunday-school teacher when she was a little girl of twelve. She is not particularly self-confident by nature, as you may have observed; and the first time she had to 'take a tray', as the phrase is, and make tea in public, there was some piteous trembling and flushing. I observed the speechless panic, the cups shaking in the little hand, and the overflowing teapot filled too full from the urn.'[4]

With this in mind, Anne's family must have been worried how she would cope with life at Roe Head, especially in light of Emily's withdrawal, but Anne herself had no such fears. This was a time for her to expand her knowledge of the world, and the people within it; it was the start of her journey into adult life, and it was a voyage she was more than ready to make.

Anne made rapid progress at Roe Head; she worked hard and diligently and soon excelled at the broad range of subjects making up the school curriculum, from history and geography to music and art. Anne, like her brother and sisters, was an accomplished artist and she loved to paint and draw. One of her finest youthful works, a portrait of Roe Head school itself was made within just a few weeks of her arrival there.

It was an auspicious start to Anne's education, but she must have been dismayed to find her relationship with

Charlotte altered. Gone was the loving sister with whom she could discuss poetry, ambitions and much more, and in her place was a teacher who remained cold and strict during school hours and aloof during their hours of leisure. Perhaps the only occasions on which their sisterly love returned during this time was the joint visits they took to the Franks' house, but at other times Charlotte was determined to keep the teacher-pupil distinction in place.

The reason for this uncharacteristic behaviour was that Charlotte was undergoing a crisis of her own at this time. Life as a teacher was very different to life as a pupil-gone were the conversations with Ellen Nussey and Mary Taylor, and in their place came long hours supervising pupils whose efforts failed to match up to Charlotte's exacting standards. She longed to write, and her hours were filled with dreams of Angria and Verdopolis, but without the time to commit them to paper they slipped away forever. These long hours in the Roe Head classroom, without the supportive friendships she had enjoyed as a pupil there, also brought back melancholy memories of the very different classrooms at Cowan Bridge. Day by day, she was slipping into one of the periods of dark depression that she had suffered from since her childhood bereavements, what she called her bilious attacks.

These feelings found some outlet in a series of letters to Ellen and in individual pieces of writing which have become known as the 'Roe Head Journal'. These were very frank and honest, and show clearly the depth of despair that Charlotte felt, as in this entry from 11th August 1836:

'All this day I have been in a dream, half miserable & half ecstatic: miserable because I could not follow it out uninterruptedly; ecstatic because it shewed almost in the vivid light of reality the ongoings of the infernal world.

I had been toiling for nearly an hour with Miss Lister, Miss Marriott & Ellen Cook, striving to teach them the difference between an article and a substantive. The parsing lesson was completed, a dead silence had succeeded it in the school-room, & I sat sinking from irritation & weariness into a kind of lethargy. The thought came over me: am I to spend the best part of my life in this wretched bondage, forcibly suppressing my rage at the idleness, the apathy and the hyperbolical & most asinine stupidity of those fat-headed oafs, and on compulsion assuming an air of kindness, patience & assiduity? I felt as if I could have written gloriously – I longed to write. The spirit of all Verdopolis, of all the mountainous North, of all the woodland West, of all the river-watered East came crowding into my mind. If I had had time to indulge it, I felt that the vague sensations of that moment would have settled down into some narrative better at least than anything I ever produced before. But just then a dolt came up with a lesson. I thought I should have vomited.'[5]

Surprised and discomfited at the different relationship she now had with her eldest sister, Anne nevertheless threw herself into her studies and her success at this is shown by the awarding of a medal to her at the end of the 1836 term, bearing the inscription, 'Prize for good conduct presented to Miss A. Brontë with Miss Wooler's kind love, Roe Head. Dec. 14th. 1846',[6] along with a book by Isaac Watts.

In her spare time at Roe Head, Anne also continued the Gondal poetry that she had previously only written with Emily by her side. This shows the close bond, alluded to by Ellen Nussey, that would always exist between them however many miles separated them, and in this time we see Anne's youthful poetry grow in power and maturity.

Poems such as 'Alexander and Zenobia', in which the Gondal heroine Zenobia is wooed by young Alexander:

'Zenobia, I never saw
A lovelier eve than this;
I never felt my spirit raised
With more unbroken bliss!
So deep the shades, so calm the hour,
So soft the breezes sigh,
So sweetly Philomel begins
Her heavenly melody.
So pleasant are the scents that rise
From flowers of loveliest hue,
And more than all – Zenobia,
I am alone with you!'[7]

In an unskilled hand this could turn into romantic verse-by-numbers, but sixteen-year-old Anne counters this with Zenobia's lament that they are soon to be parted forever. Zenobia was a recurring character in the tales of Gondal, and Anne may first have heard the name from Aunt Branwell, who would surely have shown her John Carne's 1826 book, 'Letters From The East', in which he recounts among other things the adventures of Lady Hester Stanhope, who was called 'Zenobia' during her travels across the Middle East.[8] Carne was the second cousin of Elizabeth and the Brontës' mother Maria, so he may have acted as inspiration for their own endeavours to make it into print.

Anne also found comfort from a close friend she made at the school, belying the impression some people have of Anne always being aloof. The name of this friend was Ann Cook, sister of the Ellen Cook whose grammar lesson caused Charlotte Brontë such consternation in the journal entry above. A small piece of Ann Cook's writing was discovered in 2013, and it led many to make a rather erroneous interpretation.

It is one sentence that reads, 'Pray don't forget me, my sweet little thing, AC' followed by a kiss, and it is written in pencil in Charlotte Brontë's prayerbook just above the section entitled 'Thanksgivings'. This led many to assume that the message was for Charlotte herself, which then made them question the teacher-pupil relationship between the two, but it seems clear to me that the message was for someone else who Ann Cook knew would use Charlotte's prayerbook: Anne Brontë.

The closeness of the friendship between the two Annes is revealed in a letter that Ellen Nussey sent to Elizabeth Gaskell after reading a draft of her biography of Charlotte Brontë:

'I enclose also a notice which dear C. made in a letter on the death of a young lady who was a pupil at the time Anne Brontë was at school, a pupil who attached herself to Anne B, and Anne bestowed upon her a great deal of quiet affection and genial notice. I think the young ladies friends would most probably be gratified if dear C.'s comments on her decease were inserted. They are monied and influential people in the neighbourhood, some of them not very friendly to Currer Bell's emanations. Would they not be won by her kindly thought of one of their own?'[9]

This pupil who attached herself to Anne Brontë was Ann Cook, the daughter of Thomas Cook of Dewsbury, a wealthy blanket manufacturer. This was perhaps the greatest non-familial friendship of Anne Brontë's life, but Miss Cook died tragically aged seventeen and was buried on 6th January 1840.

We see then that Anne was excelling at Roe Head, writing poetry, and making friends, and yet the poem at the head of this chapter shows a despondent supplicant, praying fervently to be saved from sin and death. It is a clue to the physical and mental breakdown that was to end Anne's time as a pupil as 1837 drew to a close.

Anne was the most devout of the Brontës and, probably following her aunt's example since childhood, she loved to study scripture, but she increasingly found that her views of it conflicted with messages that she heard in sermons. At Haworth, she would have loved to hear her father preach as he was a firm believer in God's love for mankind, but the preachers she encountered whilst at Roe Head were often of a very different kind.

Calvinism was dominating the Church of England at this time, and many Calvinist preachers, such as William Carus Wilson of Cowan Bridge infamy, believed in the very real fires of hell, to which a poor soul would be doomed if they committed any sin at any point in their life. This was obviously a very high bar to set, but thankfully the Calvinist preachers themselves were part of 'God's elect', who were pre-destined for heaven however they acted.

This interpretation of the Bible troubled Anne deeply; it nagged away at her consciousness during the day and interrupted her sleep at night, and the message was always the same: what if you are going to hell, and what if all those you love are going to hell and it is already too late to save them? Eventually these dark thoughts started to predominate and, like Emily before her, she retreated into her shell and became weaker and weaker. Charlotte, who was labouring under her own burden, failed to notice the decline in Anne as quickly as she had spotted it in Emily, and by the time the severity of Anne's condition was noticed it was almost too late.

It was found that Anne had gastric fever, what we would call typhoid today, a condition that was frequently fatal. As well as medical help, a priest was summoned, but Anne insisted that it was not one of the Calvinist priests in the area, but rather a young man named James la Trobe. La Trobe was a dissenter, one who did not attend Church of England services, who belonged to the Moravian Church. The Moravians originated in what is now the Czech Republic before moving to England to escape persecution, and the West Riding of Yorkshire was an area in which they were particularly popular.

The Taylor family of Gomersal were among many who attended Moravian churches, and it may be that Anne first heard about them from Charlotte's friend, Mary Taylor. Their beliefs were diametrically opposed to Calvinism, in that they believed in eternal salvation rather than damnation, and in a loving creator who would forgive anything and anyone. It may seem strange that these were regarded as radical beliefs among Christians in the day, but they were in accord with what Anne herself had come to believe. It was for this reason that Anne asked for a Moravian minister when she felt her own end approaching, and thankfully for us La Trobe recorded his meetings with her:

'She was suffering from a severe attack of gastric fever which brought her very low, and her voice was barely a whisper; her life hung on a slender thread. She soon got over the shyness natural on seeing a perfect stranger. The words of love, from Jesus, opened her ear to my words, and she was very grateful for my visits. I found her well acquainted with the main truths of the Bible respecting our salvation, but seeing them more through the law than the gospel, more as a requirement from God than His gift in His Son, but her heart opened to the sweet views of salvation, pardon, and peace in the blood of Christ, and, had she died then, I would have counted her His redeemed and ransomed child. It was not til I read Charlotte Brontë's 'Life' [Elizabeth Gaskell's biography] that I recognised my interesting patient at Roe Head.'[10]

With Charlotte's care and la Trobe's words to comfort her, Anne Brontë recovered, but she was sent home to Haworth to complete her recuperation in December 1837. Anne never returned to formal education, but the more than two years she spent at Roe Head is the longest period that any Brontë sibling completed at school.

Charlotte returned to the school, and continued her duties after it moved location to Heald's House in Dewsbury. She blamed, rather unfairly, Margaret Wooler for failing to spot Anne's illness and had a frank exchange with her former teacher and now employer, which left Miss Wooler in tears for two days. Charlotte's descent into illness continued apace at Dewsbury, to the extent that a doctor advised that she must leave her post or risk her life. Thus, in May 1838, Charlotte Brontë too returned to Haworth. Charlotte and Margaret Wooler eventually became friends again, to the extent that it was she who gave Charlotte away at her wedding in 1855[11] and, as we shall see, offered help to Anne at the end of her life.

Anne's years as a pupil there had made its mark on both sisters, and the battle between Calvinist doctrines and her own personal beliefs that raged so fiercely at Roe Head continued to play in Anne's mind, informing her poetry, prose and her final essay. Nevertheless, la Trobe's words had strengthened her, and never again would she fall as low as she had in her school days. She even rebuffed Calvinism directly in verse in her 1843 poem 'A Word To The Calvinists', taking direct aim against their cold-hearted sermons full of damnation and hell fire:

'And, when you, looking on your fellow men,
Behold them doomed to endless misery,
How can you talk of joy and rapture then?
May God withhold such cruel joy from me!'[12]

As Anne recovered her strength in Haworth, her mind turned to her future employment. She returned from Roe Head with more knowledge and skills than she'd had before, and knew that she could make her own way in the world as a governess. As the youngest sibling, it may be that her father and aunt continued to treat her as the baby of the family, although she was now in her late teens, and it seems likely that they tried to dissuade her from this endeavour at first. We get a clue of this in Anne's first novel *Agnes Grey*, based at least partly on Anne's exploits as a governess and with Agnes as a clear representation of Anne herself. In the novel, Agnes tells her parents of her plans to enter work:

'"I should like to be a governess."

My mother uttered an exclamation of surprise, and laughed. My sister dropped her work in astonishment, exclaiming, "You a governess, Agnes! What can you be dreaming of?"

"Well! I don't see anything so very extraordinary in it. I do not pretend to be able to instruct great girls; but surely I could teach little ones: and I should like it so much: I am so fond of children. Do let me, mamma!"

"But, my love, you have not learned to take care of

yourself yet: and young children require more judgment and experience to manage than elder ones."

"But, mamma, I am above eighteen, and quite able to take care of myself, and others too. You do not know half the wisdom and prudence I possess, because I have never been tried."[13]

Agnes won the argument, and by the time Anne too was above eighteen she also had persuaded her father and aunt to let her enter life as a governess. In April 1839 she began her post as governess to the Ingham family of Blake Hall. The locale was familiar to her, as Blake Hall was in Mirfield, just over a mile away from Roe Head School. With this in mind, it may have been Margaret Wooler, remembering the abilities of her former pupil, who recommended Anne for the position, and it is likely that Anne will have seen the Ingham family during church services she attended whilst at school.

Blake Hall was a grand, rectangular building. At the head of the household was Joshua Ingham. He was a hugely wealthy man thanks to the coal mines he owned, then in ever-growing demand because of the industrial revolution, and he also served as a Justice of the Peace. Renowned for his stern ferocity he formed a contrast to his kind and quiet wife Mary, but unfortunately for Anne his children, her charges, Joshua and Mary, took after their father's character. We shall see how her months spent at Blake Hall were almost insufferable for Anne, but she had now entered the world of work, the world of adulthood. She could not have known then that all too soon she was also to experience those other great trials of adult life: love and loss.

4: From Joy to Bitter Woe

'MAIDEN, THOU WERT thoughtless once
  Of beauty or of grace,
Simple and homely in attire
Careless of form and face.
Then whence this change, and why so oft
Dost smooth thy hazel hair?
And wherefore deck thy youthful form
With such unwearied care?
'Tell us – and cease to tire our ears
With yonder hackneyed strain –
Why wilt thou play those simple tunes
So often o'er again?'
'Nay, gentle friends, I can but say
That childhood's thoughts are gone.
Each year its own new feelings brings
And years move swiftly on,
And for these little simple airs,
I love to play them o'er –
So much I dare not promise now
To play them never more.'
I answered and it was enough;
They turned them to depart;
They could not read my secret thoughts
Nor see my throbbing heart.
I've noticed many a youthful form
Upon whose changeful face
The inmost workings of the soul
The gazer's eye might trace.

The speaking eye, the changing lip,
The ready blushing cheek,
The smiling or beclouded brow
Their different feelings speak.
But, thank God! you might gaze on mine
For hours and never know
The secret changes of my soul
From joy to bitter woe.
Last night, as we sat round the fire
Conversing merrily,
We heard without approaching steps
Of one well known to me.
There was no trembling in my voice,
No blush upon my cheek,
No lustrous sparkle in my eyes,
Of hope or joy to speak;
But O my spirit burned within,
My heart beat thick and fast.
He came not nigh – he went away
And then my joy was past.
And yet my comrades marked it not,
My voice was still the same;
They saw me smile, and o'er my face –
No signs of sadness came;
They little knew my hidden thoughts
And they will never know
The anguish of my drooping heart,
The bitter aching woe!'

('Self Congratulation', dated 1st January 1840)

When Anne Brontë arrived at Blake Hall in the spring of 1839, she was taking a step into the unknown. The only children she had ever spent any amount of time with were her siblings during her own infancy, all of whom were older than her of course, and during her service as a Sunday school teacher. She was well-liked and respected as a teacher in Haworth, despite her quiet yet serious manner, and the children were well-behaved when in her care; this may, however, have been largely because of the respect which her father commanded in the village, and because these classes represented a rare opportunity for education to those children who worked from an early age, an opportunity they were eager to grasp.

We see this respect for Anne as a teacher in first person testimonials[1] and in the semi-fictional account given by Charlotte in *Shirley*, when Caroline meets her pupils at a social gathering:

'Miss Helstone knew these girls liked her, yet she was shy with them even outside of school. They were not more in awe of her than she of them. She drew near them now, rather to find protection in their company than patronize them with her presence. By some instinct they knew her weakness, and with natural politeness they respected it. Her knowledge commanded their esteem when she taught them; her gentleness attracted their regard; and because she was what they considered wise and good when on duty, they kindly overlooked her evident timidity when off.'[2]

If Anne expected her new charges at Blake Hall to be just as respectful, and just as keen to learn, she was very mistaken. The large building she now found herself living and working in was a formidable sight, but the severe man who ran it could be just as formidable. Joshua Ingham was respected by those who relied upon his money and patronage in the Mirfield area, but despised by many others, to the extent where a violent crowd had tried to murder him just a few months before Anne arrived at Blake Hall. The riot took place following a meeting in Dewsbury in which Ingham, acting as magistrate, supported the unpopular New Poor Law which divided families and saw the poorest incarcerated in workhouses. Reports state that Ingham was hit by a heavy stone, attacked by a woman named Batty who pulled off his shoes, and then accosted by people who tried to drown him in a beck[3]. After being rescued, Ingham remained resolute; he had no interest in how the people suffered or what they had to say, and his children felt much the same about their new governess.

What dismayed Anne from the first day of her work was that the children's level of education was far below that of the working class Haworth pupils she had known. Although there were also three younger children in the Hall (Martha, Emily and baby Henrietta, known as Harriette), Anne's charges were Joshua Cunliffe (his middle name a tribute to his maternal grandfather, the local Member of Parliament) aged six and Mary aged five. It was with great surprise that Anne found that Joshua and Mary were barely able to read and write, and her reports back home to Haworth were summed up in a letter sent by Charlotte to Ellen Nussey:

'Both her pupils are desperate little dunces – neither of them can read and sometimes they even profess a profound ignorance of their alphabet. The worst of it is the little monkies (*sic*) are excessively indulged and she is not empowered to inflict any punishment.'[4]

Free of the threat of chastisement, the young Inghams ran amok in the classroom, but eight years later Anne was to inflict a different kind of punishment on them by portraying them as the cruel governess-taunting and animal-torturing Bloomfield children in *Agnes Grey*. The mood within Blake Hall took an even more sombre turn on 4th December 1839 when one-year-old Harriette died. It may be this that forced the mourning Inghams to re-assess Anne's role within their home, but it is clear that Anne had been in conflict with her charges and employers for some time. The daughter of Anne's pupil, Mary, later recalled one particular incident which had taken its place in their family folklore:

'One day grandmother, Mary Ingham, went into the school room and found two of the children tied to opposite table legs whilst Anne wrote.'[5]

By the end of 1839 Anne was back in Haworth, her employment terminated, but at least her ordeal at the hands of the Ingham children was at an end. She had left with dreams of life as a governess, but returned having seemingly proved the fears of her father and aunt right. Their must have been a burning disappointment in her heart, but as she approached the familiar Parsonage again her spirits rose at the thought of those who would be waiting for her: first and foremost Emily of course, and then Charlotte and Branwell, her father and aunt, and the kind, faithful old servant Tabby Aykroyd whom Anne had come to love like a grandmother since she had entered the Brontë home in 1824 as a replacement for the Garrs sisters.

After receiving a loving welcome as of a hero returning home from battle, it would not have taken long for her to be apprised of the latest news that had made waves in the Parsonage and Haworth as a whole. A new assistant curate had arrived while Anne was in Mirfield; his name was William Weightman and, for Anne Brontë, life would never be the same again.

The parish of Haworth was an exceptionally busy one for one priest to manage, especially because of the high mortality rate in the village, and all the funeral services that that brought with it.[6] By 1839 Patrick was in his sixties and in need of the help that an assistant curate would provide, but unfortunately without the means to pay for one. He applied to the Church Pastoral Aid Society to cover an assistant curate's wages and, having secured that, asked his Bishop to send a suitable candidate. As Patrick later recalled, the selection of William Weightman for the role was an inspired choice:

'I applied to the justly venerated apostolical Bishop of this Diocese, requesting his Lordship to send me a Curate, adequate to the wants and wishes of the parishioners. This application was not in vain. Our Diocesan, in the scriptural character of the Overlooker and Head of his Clergy, made an admirable choice, which more than answered my expectations, and probably yours.'[7]

William Weightman was the son of a merchant of Appleby, in what was then Westmorland and is now Cumbria. He arrived in August 1839, while Anne was in Mirfield, having recently completed his Master of Arts degree and licence in Theology at Durham University, the new university of the north which had only recently become England's third university after Oxford and Cambridge.

We know from Patrick's glowing funeral oration about him that William possessed a quick mind and had been an excellent scholar, and, even more importantly, was very kind-hearted and could mix easily with people of any background.

This winning combination saw him rapidly gain favour

with the parishioners of Haworth, and as demonstrated by their attacks on Samuel Redhead two decades earlier they were not easily won over. He also won the respect and admiration of Patrick, who said that from the first day they had been like father and son[8], and once again this was not always the case with the exacting Reverend Brontë and his assistant curates. Anne's first encounters with William Weightman would likely have been during the Christmas services at St. Michael's and All Angels church where he and her father worked. In the coming weeks she would have encountered him as a regular visitor to the house, and perhaps the first thing that struck her was how quickly he had made a friend in Emily. The charming newcomer had even managed to dismiss the stone-like reserve of her beloved sister, and this in itself must have been a great recommendation in Anne's eyes.

A mark of William's character came in February 1840, after he discovered that none of the Brontë sisters had ever received a Valentine's card. As the 14th approached, he purchased four cards (three for the sisters and one for Ellen Nussey who was visiting Haworth Parsonage at the time) and wrote individual verses in each of them; he then walked nine miles to Bradford to post the cards, and back again, in wintry conditions so that the postmark on the envelopes wouldn't give the identity of the sender away.

Eventually his role in the mysterious cards was discovered, but we can imagine the thrill felt by Anne, Charlotte, Emily and Ellen as they tried to work out who the mystery admirer could be. Thanks to a letter from Charlotte to Ellen looking back at the event, we know the titles of three of the cards: 'Fair Ellen, Fair Ellen', 'Soul Divine' and 'Away Fond Love'. If we make the assumption that Charlotte's letter failed to reveal the name of the verse composed to herself, and of course accept that the first verse was obviously addressed to Ellen Nussey, then the verse composed for Anne must have been either 'Soul Divine' or 'Away Fond Love'.

Anne Brontë was bruised from her first experience of life as a governess, but far from broken. She reasoned to herself that future charges could not be as uncontrollable as the Ingham children had been, and that a future employer was unlikely to be as stern as Joshua Ingham. Above all, she wanted to prove to herself and her family that she could succeed as a governess and that she could make her way in the world that lay outside the Parsonage walls. With that in mind, Anne had wasted no time in searching for a new position, and it could well be that she had placed an advertisement in a newspaper, much in the way that would-be governess Jane Eyre does in Charlotte's novel.

By May she had found a new position, and it may be that William Weightman knew of her search at the time he wrote his Valentine's verse – in which case his 'Away Fond Love' could demonstrate his feelings as he anticipated the departure of the woman he was just getting to know.

Indeed, it may even be that William Weightman himself helped to secure Anne's new position. On 8th May 1840 Anne arrived at Thorp Green Hall outside York to take up the post of governess for the Robinson family. The head of the household was Reverend Edmund Robinson, but he was a reverend in name only – having been ordained he never in fact practised as a priest other than when baptising his own children and, mysteriously, one local girl, and preferred to spend most of his time in country pursuits. His wife, Lydia, was the daughter of Reverend Thomas Gisborne, a cleric from a wealthy Staffordshire family who became Canon of Durham. In this position he was instrumental in the formation of Durham University, and his grandson, Lydia's nephew, Lionel Gisborne studied at the fledgling institution contemporaneously with William Weightman.[9]

Another co-founder of the University was Archdeacon Charles Thorp who was cousin to Reverend Edmund Robinson's father. It is more than possible then that William Weightman knew relatives of both the master and mistress of Thorp Green Hall and if, through these connections, he knew that they were looking for a governess it could have been he who recommended the daughter of his Haworth employer.

However it was that Anne gained her position, by the time that she left for the North Riding she would already have felt at least a pang of regret at the man she was leaving behind. William Weightman was everything she valued in a man; he was pious, gentle, intelligent and kind, with a hint of mischief on occasion too. He was also a very handsome man, as we can see from the portrait Charlotte made of him in 1840.

Charlotte's letters reveal sharply contrasting attitudes towards William. At first she clearly fell head over heels for him, and is teased mercilessly by Ellen for the amount of sittings she makes him endure for his portrait. She is enraptured by his first Valentine's card but by the following year, when he sends cards again, she is dismissive of him and his intentions:

'I knew better how to treat it than I did those we received a year ago. I am up to the dodges and artifices of his Lordship's character, he knows I know him, and you cannot conceive how quiet and respectful he has been. Mind I am not writing against him, I never <u>will</u> do that. I like him very much. I honour and admire his generous, open disposition, and sweet temper – but for all the tricks, wiles and insincerities of love the gentleman has not his match for 20 miles round. He would fain persuade every woman under 30 whom he sees that he is desperately in love with her. I have a great deal more to say but I have not a moment's time to write it in.'[10]

Charlotte has by this time been upset by William Weightman failing to reciprocate her feelings for him, something she would also later suffer with Constantin Heger in Brussels, but is there a particular reason that she feels spurned? A clue comes in the form of another letter from Charlotte to Ellen, this time from January 1842, three days after Anne's twenty-second birthday:

'He sits opposite Anne at church sighing softly and looking out of the corners of his eyes to win her affection – and Anne is so quiet, her looks so downcast – they are a picture.'[11]

This is one indicator that Anne Brontë and William Weightman are in love with each other, but the most compelling evidence of all is found in Anne's writing. There can be no doubt at all that Reverend Weston whom we shall meet later in *Agnes Grey* is actually Reverend Weightman, and he can also be found time and again in Anne's poetry. As we see from the poem at the head of this chapter, even in the weeks after their first meeting Anne is having to hide her emotions as she hears his steps pass by. 'Lines Written At Thorp Green' was written by Anne, unsurprisingly, during her work as governess there in August 1840 (she also wrote a further poem with the same title a year later) and in it she is forlornly longing for a visit from a man she loves. It is William Weightman she addresses in heartfelt verse:

'My life is very lonely,
My days pass heavily;
I'm weary of repining,
Wilt thou not come to me?
Oh didst thou know my longings
For thee from day to day,
My hopes so often blighted,
Thou wouldst not thus delay.'[12]

It is my belief that by the following year William did know her longings, and reciprocated them. We will never know what the future could have held for them, but it would have been expected at the time for an up-and-coming young curate like William to marry, and it would have been seen as ideal for him to select as a wife the daughter of a more experienced priest, such as Patrick Brontë. It has been said that Anne was the prettiest Brontë, her work as a governess at Thorp Green was greatly valued, showing she had all the skills a minister's wife could need, and she was the most devout of the Brontës. In short she and William Weightman were a perfect match for each other, but any plans they may have had would never come to fruition, for tragedy of the worst kind was about to strike Anne's life.

One reason that William was so loved by his parishioners was that he was renowned for visiting the sick, and for bringing them gifts paid for out of his own pocket. It was a vocation he felt called to, but a highly dangerous one in a village as disease-ridden as Haworth. He was doing just that on 14th August 1842 when his luck finally ran out – William contracted cholera from a parishioner he was visiting, declined swiftly and died aged twenty-six on 6th September 1842. By William's side was a man who had become a firm friend, Branwell Brontë, who wrote to another friend Francis Grundy:

'I have had a long attendance at the deathbed of the Rev. William Weightman, one of my dearest friends... excuse this scrawl, my eyes are too dim with sorrow to see well.'[13]

Branwell was at William's funeral on 2nd October, but Anne was far away with her grief at Thorp Green Hall. Hearing of William's death must have been a terrible ordeal for Anne – too young to comprehend the deaths of her sisters Maria and Elizabeth, or to know of her mother's passing, this was the first death of a loved one she encountered and the scars it left never healed. Even so, she may later have found some solace reading the beautiful words delivered by her father at William's memorial service.

Patrick had always preached ex tempore, without reading from a script, but so loved was William by the Haworth villagers that they asked him to write a sermon for his memorial service so that they could buy printed copies of it. This he duly did, and the proceeds from the sermon, priced at six pence each, went to the Sunday school where William had taught alongside Anne when she was on vacation from her duties with the Robinsons. It is an incredibly moving sermon in which Patrick is fulsome in his praise for the assistant curate he had lost at such a tender age:

'In his preaching, and practising, he was, as every clergyman ought to be, neither distant nor austere, timid nor obtrusive, nor bigoted, exclusive, nor dogmatical. He was affable, but not familiar; open, but not too confiding. He thought it better, and more scriptural, to make the love of God, rather than the fear of hell, the ruling motive for obedience... For about three years, our Reverend Friend in his sacred office has laboured amongst us, faithfully preaching the doctrines expressed and implied in our text, There are many, who for a short time can please, and even astonish – but, who soon retrograde and fall into disrepute. His character wore well; the surest proof of real worth. He had, it is true, some peculiar advantages. Agreeable in person and manners, and constitutionally cheerful, his first introduction was prepossessing. But what he gained at first, he did not lose afterwards. He had those qualities that enabled him to gain ground. He had classical attainments of the first order, and above all, his religious principles were sound and orthodox... He had the rare art of communicating information with diligence and strictness, without austerity, so as to render instruction, even to the youngest and most giddy, a pleasure, and not a task. The Sunday School Committee, and Teachers, as well as learners, have duly appreciated his talents in this way, and will long remember him with esteem and regret... As he was himself a friend to many, and an enemy to none, so by a kind of reaction, he had, I think I might say, no enemies and many friends... Our late lamented friend ran a bright, but short career. He died in the twenty-sixth year of his age. He had not attained the meridian of man's life; amidst the joyous, and sanguine anticipations of friends, the good wishes of all, and, as may naturally be supposed, the glad hopes of himself, he was summoned for his removal from this world to the bar of eternity... When good men die early, in the full tide of their usefulness, there is bewildering amazement, till we read in the scriptures, they are taken away from the evil to come. In all such cases, we want faith, and strong faith too.'[14]

There were two further, very telling, tributes to William Weightman. The Haworth parishioners raised money to have a plaque erected in his honour, and it can still be seen today – the largest of all the plaques in Haworth's church. The second, even more powerful, tribute came from Anne Brontë. For Anne, the idea of romantic love died with William Weightman, there would never be anyone else for her, but his passing was the catalyst not only for the hero of her first novel but for the best poetry she wrote. From the moment of William's passing, Anne began to write a series of mournful, heartfelt, beautiful poems full of love and loss. As her father's sermon said, she was being tested and she needed faith, strong faith. It was a belief that she would be re-united with William Weightman in an eternal afterlife that filled her hopes and her writing, and which solaced her somewhat through the dark days she was about to face at Thorp Green Hall and beyond.

5: Engulfed in Clouds and Rain

'I WILL NOT mourn thee, lovely one,
      Though thou art torn away.
'Tis said that if the morning sun
      Arise with dazzling ray
And shed a bright and burning beam
      Athwart the glittering main,
'Ere noon shall fade that laughing gleam
      Engulfed in clouds and rain.
And if thy life as transient proved,
      It hath been full as bright,
For thou wert hopeful and beloved;
      Thy spirit knew no blight.
If few and short the joys of life
      That thou on earth couldst know,
Little thou knew'st of sin and strife
      Nor much of pain and woe.
If vain thy earthly hopes did prove,
      Thou canst not mourn their flight;
Thy brightest hopes were fixed above
      And they shall know no blight.
And yet I cannot check my sighs,
      Thou wert so young and fair,
More bright than summer morning skies,
      But stern death would not spare;
He would not pass our darling by
      Nor grant one hour's delay,
But rudely closed his shining eye
      And frowned his smile away,

That angel smile that late so much
Could my fond heart rejoice;
And he has silenced by his touch
The music of thy voice.
I'll weep no more thine early doom,
But O! I still must mourn
The pleasures buried in thy tomb,
For they will not return.'

('To –', dated December 1842)

In the Brontë family, when tragedy came, it frequently came in multiples, so just as Maria and Elizabeth had died in rapid succession, and as Branwell and Emily would die within a handful of months of each other, so a double loss of the worst kind struck Anne Brontë in the autumn of 1842.

Still reeling from the death of William Weightman just a month previously, and the death of so many dreams along with it, a letter arrived at Thorp Green Hall in late October 1842 informing Anne that her aunt had fallen suddenly ill, and was not expected to survive.

Aunt Branwell had been like a mother to Anne, she had been with her throughout her childhood and supported and encouraged her in her adult life; she was without doubt the most important relative in Anne's life, and now, at the time she felt the need of her support and wisdom more than ever before, she was about to leave her.

There is a false perception of Elizabeth Branwell – some think that she was a severe and joyless woman who cared little for her nieces and nephew, but in fact nothing could be further from the truth. Elizabeth gave up all her hopes, her home and friends, and her riches to stay in Haworth to look after her sister's children as best she could. She was mocked for wearing old fashioned clothes, but whilst she had been a society beauty in Cornwall she forewent those pleasures in Yorkshire and used the money to support her nieces and nephew instead. Far from being dour, we hear from Ellen Nussey that she loved to joke and laugh:

'She gave one the idea that she had been a belle among her home acquaintances. She took snuff out of a very pretty gold snuff-box, which she sometimes presented to you with a little laugh, as if she enjoyed the slight shock and astonishment visible in your countenance.'[1]

Forget reports of her making her nieces sew endlessly, Elizabeth actively encouraged their creativity and love of reading, as evidenced by her Christmas present of the Scott novel, and by the fact that they engaged in so much writing throughout their childhood. Perhaps the greatest tribute of all to the true nature and character of Aunt Branwell comes from Branwell Brontë. If she really was a strict, severe woman she would surely have clashed with the free-spirited, sometimes straying, Branwell, but in actuality we see that he loved her dearly:

'I am incoherent, I fear, but I have been waking two nights witnessing such agonising suffering as I would not wish my worst enemy to endure; and I have now lost the guide and director of all the happy days connected with my childhood.'[2]

Anne obtained leave from her employers and was back in Haworth for her aunt's funeral on 3rd November, remaining at the Parsonage until she returned to Thorp Green at the end of the month. It was a time of deep mourning for Anne, as not only was she remembering Elizabeth, the mother-like figure with whom she had shared a room throughout her childhood, but also the man she had loved, William Weightman. He was buried in a crypt beneath the church floor rather than in the overcrowded churchyard, and we can tell from a poem that Anne wrote in 1844 how she must have paced over and over the floor above his final resting place:

'Yes, thou art gone! and never more
Thy sunny smile shall gladden me;
But I may pass the old church door,
And pace the floor that covers thee,
May stand upon the cold, damp stone,
And think that, frozen, lies below
The lightest heart that I have known,
The kindest I shall ever know.'[3]

Five days after Anne's mournful arrival in Haworth she at least had the comfort of two familiar and much loved faces returning too: Emily and Charlotte. Anne's sisters had been in Brussels since February, ostensibly with the intention of learning language skills that could help them attract pupils to a school the three sisters talked of opening one day. However, letters informing them of their aunt's illness and then death followed swiftly after each after and they arrived back in Yorkshire too late for the funeral of the woman who had raised them.

Anne had written of their school plans in her diary paper of July 1841:

'We are thinking of setting up a school of our own but nothing definite is settled about it yet and we do not know whether we shall be able to or not – I hope we shall.'[4]

November at Thorp Green Hall must have seemed especially bleak; Anne would never see William Weightman or her aunt again, and although Emily now remained in

Haworth to assist the ageing Tabby Aykroyd with domestic duties, Charlotte was once again in Brussels, seeing something of the world, while she herself was in the drudging routine of domestic servitude. Nevertheless Anne found some solace, as always, when alone in nature, and she particularly enjoyed a woodland near the Hall called The Long Plantation. We know this because it inspired her to write perhaps her finest poem in December 1842. Anne wrote this verse in Haworth during her Christmas break from governess duties, but as the moorland landscape of Haworth was barren of trees she is clearly thinking back to the woods around Thorp Green Hall. It had been a year of unparalleled tragedy for Anne, yet her spirit is raised by nature's wild power:

'My soul is awakened, my spirit is soaring
And carried aloft on the wings of the breeze;
For above and around me the wild wind is roaring,
Arousing to rapture the earth and the seas.
The long withered grass in the sunshine is glancing,
The bare trees are tossing their branches on high;
The dead leaves, beneath them, are merrily dancing,
The white clouds are scudding across the blue sky.
I wish I could see how the ocean is lashing
The foam of its billows to whirlwinds of spray;
I wish I could see how its proud waves are dashing,
And hear the wild roar of their thunder today!'[5]

Anne Brontë spent more than five years working as a governess to the Robinson family at Thorp Green Hall, which is far longer than any jobs that her sister or brother held, and yet her writing at this time reveals the frustration and despair that she often felt during that time. In her 1841 diary paper, she comments frankly, 'I am a governess in the family of Mr Robinson. I dislike the situation and wish to change it for another.'[6]

Just what was it that made Anne dislike this position so much, for in many ways she found herself in a very different environment to the one she had encountered at Mirfield's Blake Hall? Anne was placed in charge of three pupils, Lydia junior, Elizabeth (known as Bessie) and her youngest pupil Mary, who was twelve at the time of Anne's arrival. They were significantly older than her Ingham charges had been, and they were better educated and far better behaved.

Despite her personal unhappiness, Anne thrived in this second governess role, and a sign of the esteem in which her pupils held her came when they presented her with a gift that she truly loved: a Cavalier King Charles Spaniel puppy which she named Flossy. From 1843 Anne could walk the North Riding landscape with Flossy by her side, and he also accompanied her back to Haworth during her vacations, and during the annual summer sojourn to Scarborough.

Scarborough was one of England's most fashionable resorts at a time when overseas travel was the preserve of the wealthy, and it attracted some of the leading families from across the north of the country. They were there to see and to be seen, and to have their attendance recorded in the local newspapers; this was the cream of northern society, and the Robinsons of Thorp Green Hall were at their vanguard. Thankfully for Anne, she was expected to attend too, and she quickly fell in love with its golden sands, its luxurious spa complex and its series of concerts held nightly. Above all, as we saw from 'Lines Composed In A Wood On A Windy Day', she loved stormy nights when the waves crashed against the rocks of the town's south and north bays.

Anne spent around six weeks of the year in Scarborough during the summer months of 1840 to 1844, so that, for example, in 1842 we know that she arrived with the Robinsons on 4th July and left on 15th August, staying at 15, The Cliff, an exclusive location which was part of Wood's Lodgings. Wood's Lodgings no longer exists, but the imposing Grand Hotel stands on the spot today, offering the same striking views across Scarborough's south bay. Don't be misled by its name, for in fact Wood's Lodgings provided luxurious accommodation used by the elite visitors to the town. Another family known to Anne were also in Wood's Lodgings in that summer of 1842: the Inghams of Blake Hall. No doubt Anne breathed a sigh of relief when she compared the family she had left to the one she was now employed by.

These Scarborough summers provided some of the happiest days in Anne Brontë's life, with fine music, sunny strolls, and an opportunity to step back in time by visiting the imposing castle or the Rotunda Museum dedicated to geology and natural history. All too soon, however, these carefree weeks passed, to be replaced by careworn months in the Thorp Green classroom.

One reason that Anne found her situation at Thorp Green so melancholic was that she missed her family, and she missed the familiar Parsonage of Haworth and the moors stretching away from it. The grand hall she lived in now, larger even than Blake Hall, with its extensive grounds was no match for the old building she knew and loved, as we can see from this poem with its poignantly capitalised final word:

'How brightly glistening in the sun
The woodland ivy plays!
While yonder beeches from their barks
Reflect his silver rays.
That sun surveys a lovely scene
From softly smiling skies;
And wildly through unnumbered trees
The wind of winter sighs:
Now loud, it thunders o'er my head,
And now in distance dies.
But give me back my barren hills
Where colder breezes rise;
Where scarce the scattered, stunted trees
Can yield an answering swell,
But where a wilderness of heath
Returns the sound as well.
For yonder garden, fair and wide,
With groves of evergreen,
Long winding walks, and borders trim,
And velvet lawns between;
Restore to me that little spot,
With grey walls compassed round,
Where knotted grass neglected lies,
And weeds usurp the ground.
Though all around this mansion high
Invites the foot to roam,
And though its halls are fair within –
Oh, give me back my HOME!'[7]

At the start of 1843, as Anne prepared to return to Thorp
Green from Christmas in Haworth, she must have felt
in a more positive mood than usual on such occasions,
for travelling with her was her brother Branwell. The

Robinsons had decided that their son Edmund, named after his father and then eleven years of age, needed a male tutor rather than being taught by Anne on occasion alongside his sisters. So highly did they value Anne's work and judgement that they asked if she knew a man who would be suitable for the role, and once again her thoughts turned to home.

Branwell had by this time tried to become a portrait painter in Bradford, but found competition too fierce and clients too scarce, and had been dismissed from a potentially lucrative role as station master at Luddendenfoot railway station near Halifax. Unfortunately, Branwell spent more time writing and drinking with friends than supervising his staff, and when one was accused of misappropriating monies, it was Branwell who was found guilty of 'constant and culpable carelessness'[8] and dismissed.

After leaving the railways in March 1842, Branwell had succumbed once more to heavy drinking and opium use, but Anne still had faith in him. She knew his kind heart and remembered how he had drawn pictures for her and led their childhood excursions onto the moors; she knew too that he possessed a brilliant mind, and had received an excellent education from her father. When Anne suggested that her brother would be a suitable tutor for young Edmund, the Robinsons were quick to agree the appointment, but when Branwell arrived alongside Anne in January 1843 it marked a turning point for both families.

Branwell Brontë, unlike the introverted Anne and the rest of his sisters, loved to hold court in front of an audience, and he could sometimes be found in the inns of Haworth performing his party piece: writing two different letters at the same time, with a pen in each hand. He was a great talker, and a charming man, and it seems that it did not take long for him to fall in love with the lady of the house, Lydia Robinson. In March 1843, Anne and Branwell had a welcome visitor to Thorp Green Hall in the person of their father, who was in York as a witness in a court case. Patrick reported back to Charlotte, then still in Brussels, that her brother was fitting in well and 'in good odour' with his employers, but his closeness to one particular employer would prove his downfall.

We will never know the true extent of Lydia's feelings for him, but he believed that she loved him dearly, as a letter he sent to Francis Grundy in 1845, looking back at his time at Thorp Green Hall, reveals:

'This lady (though her husband detested me) showed me a degree of kindness which, when I was deeply grieved one day at her husband's conduct, ripened into declarations of more than ordinary feeling. My admiration of her personal and mental attractions, my knowledge of her unselfish sincerity, her sweet temper, and unwearied care for others, with but unrequited return where most should have been given – although she is seventeen years my senior, all combined to an attachment on my part, and led to reciprocations which I had little looked for. During nearly three years I had daily "troubled pleasure, soon chastised by fear".'[9]

Now we see the full extent of the difficulties Anne faced as she went about her daily work. Reverend Edmund Robinson was a choleric man who showed his wife little affection and was often angry towards her, subjecting her to violent rants, and perhaps worse. Under these circumstances she turned for affection towards the young governor Branwell Brontë, leaving Anne to ignore the evidence she saw daily of this, or, even worse, attempt to cover it up to protect her brother. It could not continue.

Anne resigned her post at Thorp Green Hall, despite the protestations of her adoring pupils, in June 1845, stating that the children were now older and no longer in need of her lessons. The diary paper she wrote in the following month, however, gives a rather different view of her exit:

'I was then [looking back to her previous diary paper of 1841] at Thorp Green and now I am only just escaped from it. I was wishing to leave then and if I had known that I had four years longer to stay how wretched I should have been too. I was writing the fourth volume of Sophala but during my stay I have had some very unpleasant and undreamt of experience of human nature.'[10]

Climbing into the carriage that took her away from Thorp Green Hall, Flossy alongside her, Anne would see sadness etched on the faces of the Robinson charges for whom she was more than simply a governess, she was someone whom they respected, maybe even loved. It was not the end of Anne's association with them however, for in December 1848 two of the girls, Bessie and Mary, who by that time had married and become Mrs Clapham, arrived at Haworth Parsonage in person to see her. This journey in the heart of winter to the bleak moors of Haworth shows the depth of affection they had for Anne. Charlotte gave a touching account of what must have been a moving meeting for Anne, Bessie and Mary,[11] as at this dark time of tragedy in the Parsonage, as we shall see, they must surely have known they would never see each other again.

Anne returned to Haworth in low spirits, but her beloved Emily was there to comfort and support her, as always, and they planned to journey through York to Scarborough. Now aged twenty-five and twenty-seven respectively, this was to be Anne and Emily's first holiday together, but Anne's spirits were too downcast to enjoy thoughts of Scarborough, and after a short stay in York they returned to Haworth. Nevertheless, Emily was exalted to be in her younger sister's company once more, and as we can see from her 1845 diary paper, she hoped that they could return to writing Gondal adventures once again as if the last ten years had never happened:

'Anne and I went on our first long journey by ourselves together, leaving home on the 30th of June, Monday sleeping at York, returning to Keighley Tuesday evening, sleeping there and walking home on Wednesday morning. Though the weather was broken we enjoyed ourselves very much except during a few hours at Bradford and during our excursion we were Ronald Macelgin, Henry Angora, Juliet Angusteena, Rosabelle, Ella and Julian Egramont, Catherine Navarre and Cordelia Fitzaphnold escaping from the palaces of Instruction to join the Royalists who are hard driven at present by the victorious Republicans.'[12]

These latter named characters were all from the land of Gondal, but for Anne real-world ennui had overcome her youthful delight in the imaginary kingdom, and perhaps it was this that caused the unhappy few hours in Bradford. Nevertheless, Anne and Emily could never argue for long, and back in the comfort of the Haworth home she had longed for, Anne did return to penning Gondal verse.

Emily was not the only familiar face waiting for Anne after her return from Thorp Green. Charlotte had arrived home from Brussels on New Year's Day 1845, with a certificate of education but a shattered heart. The story is well known of how Charlotte fell in love with her tutor and then colleague Constantin Heger, husband of the woman,

Clare, who ran the Pensionnat in which Charlotte worked. Her love was not reciprocated, and the long string of plaintive letters she sent to Constantin from Haworth went unanswered. It was a bitter blow for Charlotte, but from her personal tragedy came the great heroes of her novels, all modelled, to some extent, on Monsieur Heger.

Just a month after Anne's arrival, Branwell Brontë too left Thorp Green Hall, but the timing was not of his choosing. The reasons for Branwell's sacking remain unproven, but it seems likely that without Anne's guidance his affair with Lydia Robinson had been discovered, leading to his ignominious dismissal.

All four Brontë siblings were now back in Haworth, and all but Emily were dejected and broken in spirit. For the three sisters the only option was to try to launch their own school, and they had prospectuses printed and distributed for the 'Misses Brontës' Establishment for the Board and Education of a Limited Number of Young Ladies, The Parsonage, Haworth near Bradford'. In fact the numbers were rather more limited than they hoped for, and they failed to attract a single pupil. They had tried everything and failure seemed to greet them at every turn, but fate was about to take a more benign hand after Charlotte made a chance discovery that changed literary history forever.

6: Full of Hope, and Free From Care

'WHY SHOULD SUCH gloomy silence reign;
 And why is all the house so drear,
When neither danger, sickness, pain,
Nor death, nor want have entered here?
We are as many as we were
That other night, when all were gay,
And full of hope, and free from care;
Yet, is there something gone away.
The moon without as pure and calm
Is shining as that night she shone;
but now, to us she brings no balm,
For something from our hearts is gone.
Something whose absence leaves a void,
A cheerless want in every heart.
Each feels the bliss of all destroyed
And mourns the change – but each apart.
The fire is burning in the grate
As redly as it used to burn,
But still the hearth is desolate
Till Mirth and Love with Peace return.
'Twas Peace that flowed from heart to heart
With looks and smiles that spoke of Heaven,
And gave us language to impart
The blissful thoughts itself had given.
Sweet child of Heaven, and joy of earth!
O, when will Man thy value learn?
We rudely drove thee from our hearth,
And vainly sigh for thy return.'

('Monday Night May 11ᵗʰ 1846', dated as per the title)

There were a number of reasons that the Haworth Parsonage school scheme, once the great hope of Anne and her sisters, came to nothing. Haworth was a remote village not yet connected to the ever-expanding railway system, and it was also a famously unhealthy village prone to epidemics of typhus, cholera and whooping cough. The school fee which they set at £35 per year, with extra fees payable for lessons in languages, music and drawing, was also rather expensive considering that their school had no history, and therefore no reputation. Ultimately the school failed to gain any interest, and as Anne wrote in her 1845 diary paper:

'When the last paper was written we were thinking of setting up a school – the scheme has been dropped and long after taken up again and dropped again because we could not get pupils.'[1]

Even if pupils had been found, the sisters would have faced another problem in the shape of their brother Branwell. Already in a state of despair after his dismissal from Thorp Green Hall, and separation from the woman he loved, Branwell was further agitated in May 1846 by news that the master of the Hall, Reverend Edmund Robinson, had died suddenly. Branwell, dreamer that he was, felt that Lydia would now resume their relationship, and, as he stated in a letter to Francis Grundy, he even hoped that she would now become Mrs Brontë, but in his naivety he failed to consider the social and class divide between them. Perhaps wary of Branwell's passions, Lydia now arranged for him to be told that Edmund's Will strictly forbade any contact between his widow and the governor that he had dismissed. The coachman who brought this unwelcome news to Branwell also informed him that the trustee of the Will was one Charles Thorp, and that he had threatened to shoot Branwell if he ever saw him again.[2] This was, of course, the Charles Thorp of Durham Cathedral and University who had been known to William Weightman.

The threat from Thorp may have been real, but the clause in the Will certainly was not. No such clause existed, it was simply Lydia Robinson's way of keeping Branwell out of her life at what had become a time of promise for her. Always looking for opportunities to climb the social ladder, in November 1848 she became Lady Lydia Scott after marrying Sir Edward Dolman Scott, a baronet who had himself been widowed just three months earlier.

Branwell's disillusionment and despair increased throughout the rest of his life, and he turned with ever-increasing ferocity to alcohol and laudanum. Whether the course of his life would have run differently had he never met Lydia Robinson we shall never know, but it is certain that whilst he could be a disruptive presence in Haworth Parsonage in his later years, Anne never ceased loving him. His friend Francis Grundy later blamed Branwell's decline and demise on his ill-starred love affair, and the sorrows resulting from it, although he was also at pains to defend his name against some of the charges that Elizabeth Gaskell and others had raised against him:

'I have always been of opinion that it remained for me to clear his name from the weight of accusation heaped upon it. I knew him, and indeed, I believe, all his family better than Mrs Gaskell did. He was a dear old friend, who from the rich storehouse of his memory taught me much... More sinned against, mayhap, than sinning, at *least* he proved the reality of his sorrows. They killed him.'[3]

So it was that the Parsonage which had once seemed so warm and full of promise was a drear place by the latter half of 1845; all four of the Brontë siblings had tried to secure jobs and future roles for themselves in life, all to a greater or lesser extent had failed (although Anne at least had shown that she could succeed in a workplace) – what could they do now? The answer came with the chance discovery, or possibly not-so-chance discovery, made by Charlotte Brontë which she later described in detail:

'One day, in the autumn of 1845, I accidentally lighted on a manuscript volume of verse in my sister Emily's handwriting. Of course, I was not surprised, knowing that she could and did write verse: I looked it over, and something more than surprise seized me, – a deep conviction that these were not common effusions, nor at all like the poetry women generally write. I thought them condensed and terse, vigorous and genuine. To my ear, they also had a peculiar music – wild, melancholy, and elevating.'[4]

Could it be that this discovery was not as accidental as Charlotte's account suggests, that she had in fact seen Emily secrete some papers away and at an opportune moment went to look at what had been hidden? Whatever the truth of this discovery it caused a furious argument in the Brontë household, but the world of literature would never be the same again. Emily had been writing Gondal-related poetry since her childhood, and sharing it with her sisters as a matter of course. She had also, however, been writing deeply personal poetry about life, faith, despair and death in which she laid bare her deepest emotions, and these verses had been kept secret even from Anne.

It was Emily's personal, hidden poetry that Charlotte found on that fateful day, and she was amazed at how powerful they were, at the genius so evident within their lines and stanzas. Charlotte realised at once that these poems were as good as anything being printed at the time, and that they deserved a wider audience. She attempted to persuade Emily to send them to a publisher, but to do so she also had to reveal that she had found and then read her secreted book of verse. Emily was shy and taciturn by nature, but on occasion she could be roused to a fiery temper and she now left Charlotte in no doubt of her feelings. For Emily it was a devastating discovery, her innermost thoughts and desires had been displayed before her sisters, and the sister she had long looked up to as leader of their sibling unit wanted to place those same intimate verses before the public. Doors were slammed, voices and maybe more were raised, to be succeeded by days of silence punctuated only by the mournful ticking of the grandfather clock in the middle of the Parsonage stairway.

This strained atmosphere is captured perfectly in Anne's poem that she simply titled with the date and time of its composition, and which features at the head of this chapter. Charlotte later renamed this poem 'Domestic Peace',[5] and yet it is clear that whilst the house is silent, it is far from peaceful. Thankfully for those living within the Parsonage, and for lovers of literature ever since, Anne came to the rescue, as we see when we continue to read Charlotte's recollection:

'My youngest sister quietly produced some of her own compositions, intimating that since Emily's had given me pleasure, I might like to look at hers. I could not but be a partial judge, yet I thought that these verses too had a sweet sincere pathos of their own.'[6]

Anne had been forced to take sides in this sororal argument, and she had perhaps surprisingly, on the surface, sided with Charlotte. Anne knew more than anyone how talented Emily was, however, and she too must have felt that her verse deserved to be published and read. It can also be said, taking her extended period of work at Thorp Green as evidence, that Anne was the most practical of the siblings; she realised that their chances of finding suitable life-long employment was small, but she also had belief in the power of their writing, and she now revealed her plan of embarking upon a collective literary venture.

After producing her work, Anne explained that she felt that they could compile a book made of poetry by all three sisters, rather than just by Emily alone. Anne had correctly calculated that Emily would be loathe to veto a plan from the sister she loved more than anyone else in the world, and the fact that they were once more working on a joint creative project brought back memories of the times that Anne, Charlotte, Emily and Branwell had walked round and round their dining table, composing lines out loud and discussing shared plot lines. Branwell, alas, was in neither the physical nor mental shape to join in their adult labours and the sisters agreed to keep their endeavours from him, as Charlotte later revealed:

'My unhappy brother never knew what his sisters had done in literature – he was not aware that they had ever published a line; we could not tell him of our efforts for fear of causing him too deep a pang of remorse for his own time misspent, and talents misapplied. Now he will <u>never</u> know. I cannot dwell longer on the subject at present; it is too painful.'[7]

Anne's bold move in producing her own poetry and suggesting that they try to have a collection of verse published healed the rift within the Parsonage, and softened Emily's anger; it was now time for the work to begin in earnest, and one of their first tasks was to decide upon pen names. In Charlotte's biographical notice of her sisters, published in 1850, she states that they chose male-sounding pseudonyms because publishers and critics were prejudiced against female writers. Tantalisingly, however, none of the sisters explained how they came to their eventual names, but I believe that there are three convincing, and revealing, inspirations for the choices.

Charlotte, Emily and Anne Brontë retained their initials and transformed themselves into Currer, Ellis and Acton Bell. Charlotte's choice of Currer seems to have been a mark of gratitude to Frances Mary Richardson Currer, the wealthy owner of Eshton Hall near Skipton. Frances was a well known philanthropist, supporting many institutions including Scarborough's Rotunda Museum that was surely visited by Anne during her summer weeks there. The Rotunda was, and still is, known for its geology and natural history exhibitions, subjects that Anne was fascinated with. We shall see how she read extensively on the subject and how she wrote on it too, and amidst the highlights of the Brontë Parsonage Museum today is Anne's treasured pebble collection taken from Scarborough's beaches. More pertinently, Frances was well known for providing financial support to members of the clergy in need. It was she who sent Patrick Brontë a cheque for the very generous amount of fifty pounds after the death of his wife Maria, and whose largesse he referred to in a letter to his friend Reverend John Buckworth:

'What is perhaps not less wonderful than all, a few days ago, I got a letter containing a bank post bill of the value of fifty pounds which was sent to me by a benevolent individual, a wealthy lady, in the West Riding of Yorkshire.'[8]

Patrick had spent all the money he had on fruitless medical treatments for his wife during her final illness and without the help of his friends, and of the benevolent Frances Currer, it is likely that he would have faced bankruptcy. Her kindness was evidently remembered by Patrick and his family, and so it was that Charlotte Brontë later adopted her name to write behind.

Emily's choice of Ellis has proven harder for some people to place, but to me it seems a simple and moving tribute to the elder sister Elizabeth, the kind, caring, sensible sibling who had died when Emily was just eight years old. Behind Emily's characteristic reserve beat a large heart, and she never forgot a kind deed done for her. She kept Elizabeth Brontë forever in her heart, and adopted the shortened form of her name, Ellis, when it came to her writing.

Some have claimed that Eliza Acton is the inspiration behind Anne Brontë's chosen pen name of Acton Bell. Eliza was a highly popular writer in the early nineteenth century, famed for her poetry and especially for her writing on the subject of cookery. Eliza's work appeared in the magazines that the Brontës read, but was her poetry dazzling enough to capture Anne's attention? It seems more likely to me that Anne's pseudonym is a tribute to a lost and loved family member. Acton Castle is on the outskirts of Penzance in Cornwall, and could then be seen from the Chapel Street home that Aunt Branwell had lived in before coming to Haworth. Perhaps it once formed part of the bedtime stories related by the aunt to the young niece who shared her room? By choosing Acton as a pen name, Anne was remembering her aunt, her mother and her own Cornish roots.

The pen names were agreed upon, and now it remained to select the poems to include in the collection. Anne, as Acton, contributed twenty-one, as did Emily, and Charlotte contributed nineteen, although as her poems tended to be far longer than those of her sisters there are more 'Currer Bell' words in the collection than any other.

Anne's first poem in the book that came to be known as *Poems by Currer, Ellis and Acton Bell* is 'A Reminiscence', beginning with 'Yes, thou art gone!', which we looked at in the previous chapter. It seems fitting that Anne's first contribution should also be a celebration of the life of William Weightman, as even at this point, four years after his death, he continued to influence her life, thoughts and writing.

It was a dramatic opening from Anne, and the collection as a whole showcases some of her greatest verse. Whilst Emily is widely regarded as the best Brontë poet, Anne shows in *Poems by Currer, Ellis and Acton Bell* that she could write poems of brilliance too, and that she also deserves to be remembered as one of the greatest female poets of the nineteenth century. Anne is not afraid to bare her soul in her poetry, as is amply demonstrated by 'The Arbour', the second of her poems in the collection. It begins with the narrator sitting in an arbour with the sun smiling at her through gaps in the trees. Throughout four and a half stanzas we are given an idyllic scene, but then the mood shifts dramatically to reveal the true nature of the scene, and the true nature of Anne's feelings as she wrote the poem:

'Oh, list! 'tis summer's very breath
That gently shakes the rustling trees –
But look! the snow is on the ground –
How can I think of scenes like these?
'Tis but the frost that clears the air,
And gives the sky that lovely blue;
They're smiling in a winter's sun,
Those evergreens of sombre hue.
And winter's chill is on my heart –

> How can I dream of future bliss?
> How can my spirit soar away,
> Confined by such a chain as this?'[9]

The chains that bind Anne in an icy grip are the eternal bonds of love for the man who was lying under the church floor, just a few steps from the Parsonage where she composed her poems. Her words are searingly honest, although often covered with a mourning veil as in another Acton poem within the collection, 'Appeal':

> 'Oh, I am very weary,
> Though tears no longer flow;
> My eyes are tired of weeping,
> My heart is sick of woe;
> My life is very lonely,
> My days pass heavily,
> I'm weary of repining,
> Wilt thou not come to me?
> Oh, didst thou know my longings
> For thee, from day to day,
> My hopes, so often blighted,
> Thou wouldst not thus delay!'[10]

Anne composed this poem in August 1840, and as we saw earlier, its original title was 'Lines Written at Thorp Green'. It is not hard to imagine whom Anne was repining for at this time and place; perhaps she hoped William would call at the Hall, he did have connections with the family, en route to his home county Westmorland or to an ecclesiastical engagement? By the time it was chosen to appear in the sisters' book, it had taken on a very different meaning. Anne still repined, her days were now heavier than ever, but she knew now that the cause of the delay would be insurmountable.

It may seem from these examples that Anne's poetry was relentlessly morbid, and that her life by this time was unfailingly sad, but with Anne's very last lines in the collection we see a ray of hope. It is Anne, under her Acton mask, who was chosen to close the book with 'Fluctuations'. In it, we see a series of natural phenomena that at first appear to be cheerful but are quickly supplanted by a darker reality, in similar fashion to 'The Arbour', but on this occasion Anne ends on a more upbeat note:

> 'Anon, an earthly meteor blazed
> The gloomy darkness through;
> I smiled, yet trembled while I gazed –
> But that soon vanished too!
> And darker, drearier fell the night
> Upon my spirit then; –
> But what is that faint struggling light?
> Is it the Moon again?
> Kind Heaven! increase that silvery gleam,
> And bid these clouds depart,
> And let her soft celestial beam
> Restore my fainting heart!'[11]

Anne is turning to her faith and by doing so finds life, hope and happiness, as she so often did throughout her life. It was with hope and faith that she, Emily and Charlotte parcelled together the manuscript that concluded with the above poem and sent it out into the world. As so many writers have discovered before and since, the only thing worse than waiting for a response from a publisher was receiving a terse rejection note or getting no reply at all. Charlotte later recalled this period of declining hope in their poetic venture:

'The bringing out of our little book was hard work. As was to be expected, neither we nor our poems were at all wanted... the great puzzle lay in the difficulty of getting answers of any kind from the publishers to whom we applied.'[12]

In desperation the sisters wrote for advice to Chambers of Edinburgh, who published a periodical entitled 'Information For The People'. True to their name, they wrote back to the Parsonage with some pertinent information, advising them to submit their manuscript to Aylott and Jones of London who were known for publishing poetry alongside their main business as a stationer.

There must have been mixed emotions when a reply came back from the publisher agreeing to accept the work. It is easy to imagine the excitement that Charlotte and Anne must have felt; they had long loved poetry, and now they had the chance to be published poets themselves. Emily, on the other hand, must have felt trepidation at the thought that her most private words would be exposed to the world, even if it was behind a pseudonym. Another problem was that Aylott and Jones would only publish it on the sisters' account, meaning that they had to pay the printing and publicity costs. The initial fee was £37 18s. 6d.,[13] a substantial sum that would have been far beyond their means just a few years earlier. By 1846, however, they had a legacy from Aunt Branwell to call upon, as she had left them around three hundred pounds each in her will four years earlier.[14] Could they risk this money? It was a big risk, but on the other hand, could they turn down the opportunity to fulfil a lifelong dream? Thankfully for lovers of literature, they paid the money and by June 1846 the Bell brothers had announced them-selves to the world; *Poems by Currer, Ellis and Acton Bell* was published.

If Anne and her sisters now dreamt of overnight success as poets they were to be very disappointed. A year later we find Charlotte sending copies of the book to leading writers of the day, such as Alfred Tennyson and Thomas de Quincey, with a letter stating:

'My relatives, Ellis and Acton Bell and myself, heedless of the repeated warnings of various respectable publishers, have committed the rash act of publishing a volume of poems. The consequences predicted have, of course, over-taken us; our book is found to be a drug; no man needs it or heeds it; in the space of a year our publisher has disposed of but two copies, and by what painful efforts he succeeded in disposing of those two, himself only knows.'[15]

It seems likely to me that this lack of sales, and the draining of their aunt's legacy in the process, reignited a momentary feud between Charlotte and Anne again, and it is this that caused the tense atmosphere of the night of May 11th 1846 referred to in Anne's poem of that name, just a month before they wrote to de Quincey and others. They could have been fatally discouraged by this lack of success, their writing endeavours could have ended there and we would never have heard of the Brontë name. Anne, Charlotte and Emily were made of sterner stuff, however, and this initial failure was about to spur them on to a magnificent triumph.

7: The Labours of the Day

'I HAVE SLEPT upon my couch
But my spirit did not rest,
For the labours of the day
Yet my weary soul opprest.
And before my dreaming eyes
Still the learned volumes lay,
And I could not close their leaves
And I could not turn away.
While the grim preceptors laughed
And exulted in my woe:
Till I felt my tingling frame
With the fire of anger glow.
But I oped my eyes at last,
And I heard a muffled sound,
'Twas the night breeze come to say
That the snow was on the ground.
Then I knew that there was rest
On the mountain's bosom free;
So I left my fevered couch
And I flew to waken thee.
I have flown to waken thee
For, if thou wilt not arise,
Then my soul can drink no peace
From these holy moonlight skies.
And this waste of virgin snow
To my sight will not be fair
Unless thou wilt smiling come,
Love, to wander with me there.

Then awake! Maria, wake!
For if thou couldst only know
How the quiet moonlight sleeps
On this wilderness of snow
And the groves of ancient trees
In their snowy garb arrayed,
Till they stretch into the gloom
Of the distant valley's shade.
O, I know thou wouldst rejoice
To inhale this bracing air,
Thou wouldst break thy sweetest sleep
To behold a scene so fair.
O'er these wintry wilds, *alone*,
Thou wouldst joy to wander free;
And it will not please thee less,
Though that bliss be shared with me.'

('The Student's Serenade', dated February 1844)

Whilst sales of *Poems by Currer, Ellis and Acton Bell* were disappointing, to say the least, it had attracted good reviews, and we know that one of the two purchasers of the book, a Mr Enoch, liked it so much that he wrote to the publisher asking for the autographs of the authors. It is thanks to him that the signatures of the sisters as Currer Bell, Ellis Bell and Acton Bell are preserved for posterity at the Brontë Parsonage Museum.

In light of the book's failure in commercial terms, a discussion was needed between Anne and her sisters about what course to take next; they could not afford to make another such outlay with nothing to show for it, and yet the act of setting out on their writing adventure had brought a light into their lives that would otherwise be missing. They were all mourning lost loved ones, all facing a future without any obvious career presenting itself to them, Branwell was in a state of decline and depression, and their ageing father was living in a very real darkness because of cataracts in his eyes. In these less than auspicious circumstances they needed to cling to any joy they could find in their lives and, as Charlotte described, it was this that informed their next, fateful, decision:

'Ill-success failed to crush us: the mere effort to succeed had given a wonderful zest to existence; it must be pursued. We each set to work on a prose tale.'[1]

The first love of the Brontës, and their first published work, was poetry, but the glory days when poetry attracted large sales were gone and even Wordsworth's work now sold far less than it once had. In such a market what chance did three unknown writers, the Bells, have? Literary tastes were changing and Anne and her sisters were smart enough to realise the way the wind now blew; novels were in vogue, so they duly vowed to redouble their efforts within a prose medium.

Once again they decided to work on the project together, just as they had done as children, and to seek publication in a joint collection. Completing a one volume novel each would allow them to be packaged together in a three volume set – the 'triple decker' – which was popular with publishers and the public alike. Emily produced the mighty *Wuthering Heights* from her genius imagination, partly inspired by a real life family feud connected with Law Hill in Halifax, where she had served as a teacher for six months in 1838 and 1839. Charlotte was less successful with her contribution – *The Professor* follows the adventures of an Englishman who falls in love while serving as a teacher in a Brussels school. Clearly, an unrequited love for Monsieur Heger, her former Professor and then colleague in Brussels, still burned fiercely within Charlotte, but whilst there are some nice touches and excellent writing within *The Professor*, it would be put to much better use in Charlotte's later Belgian-based masterpiece *Villette*.

Anne's novel was eventually given the title of *Agnes Grey*, but her 1845 diary paper reveals that it may once have had a very different name, and that Anne may have already been working on it for some time before the prose project was decided upon:

'I have begun the third volume of passages in the life of an Individual. I wish I had finished it.'[2]

It has been suggested that this 'life of an Individual' is what eventually became Anne's first novel, as whilst it is a relatively slim book it does have three distinct sections: life as a governess with the Bloomfields, life with the Murrays, and life as a teacher at her mother's school. It is also easy to imagine why Anne should have found this third volume difficult to write, for if the work referred to is indeed *Agnes Grey*, in the final section she unveils her deepest dreams and confronts her greatest loss.

If, as I and many others believe, the 'life of an Individual' later became the life of Agnes Grey, then we should also recognise that at many points the life of Agnes Grey portrayed in the eponymous novel closely mirrored the life of Anne Brontë.

Autobiographical elements can often be found in great works of fiction, and they appear regularly in all Brontë novels, so that we can easily see Charlotte as both Jane Eyre and Lucy Snowe, and Shirley Keeldar and Caroline Helstone of Charlotte's novel *Shirley* are clearly based at least in part upon Emily and Anne. *Agnes Grey*, however, is by far the most autobiographical of any of the sisters' books, and we get a clue as to the nature of what is to follow from Anne's very first line:

'All true histories contain instruction; though, in some, the treasure may be hard to find, and when found, so trivial in quantity, that the dry, shrivelled kernel scarcely compensates for the trouble of cracking the nut. Whether this be the case with my history or not, I am hardly competent to judge. I sometimes think it might prove useful to some, and entertaining to others; but the world may judge for itself. Shielded by my own obscurity, and by the lapse of years, and a few fictitious names, I do not fear to venture; and will candidly lay before the public what I would not disclose to the most intimate friend.'[3]

This is ostensibly Agnes preparing to tell her story, but after the lapse of a few, two hundred or so, years we can now see past a few fictitious names and observe that it's also Anne preparing to tell her own story. She has broken down the fourth wall and is addressing the reader directly in an almost post-modern fashion.

This continues in the second paragraph in which the narrator reveals that she is the daughter of a clergyman of the North of England, a man from a poor family yet who married a woman from a far more exalted social background. So far, so Brontë, and Anne continues to make full use of her life experiences to create a novel that is slender yet incredibly moving, and which rewards reading time and time again.

Agnes' father runs into money difficulties and so our heroine decides to strike out and make her own way in the world as a governess. What follows is a tale of service in two very different families, yet two very familiar ones to those who know Anne's story.

Her first post is at Wellwood House, where she works for the Bloomfield family, a thinly veiled portrait of the Inghams of Blake Hall. Agnes finds that Mrs Bloomfield is kind but refuses to discipline her children, whereas the master of the house Mr Bloomfield is a stern disciplinarian whose children also exhibit a cruel streak. Just as we know from Charlotte's letter that Anne's pupils at Ingham Hall were 'desperate little dunces', we find Agnes's Wellwood pupils to have the same deficiencies:

'I found my pupils very backward, indeed; but Tom, though averse to every species of mental exertion, was not without abilities. Mary Ann could scarcely read a word, and was so careless and inattentive that I could hardly get on with her at all.'[4]

Tom Bloomfield is an especially objectionable child who likes nothing better than torturing birds, and he and Mary Ann's schoolroom repertoire include spitting in Agnes's bag and throwing its contents out of the window. Perhaps behaviour of this kind is the reason that Anne Brontë resorted to tying her Ingham charges to table legs?

Agnes is soon dismissed from Wellwood House, just as Anne was from Blake Hall, but like her creator the fictional governess refuses to be downhearted and soon finds another position, although this new adventure will take her further away from her parsonage home than ever before:

'It was decreed that on the last day of January, I was to enter upon my new office as governess in the family of Mr Murray, of Horton Lodge, near O-, about seventy miles from our village, a formidable distance to me, as I had never been above twenty miles from home in all the course of my twenty years' sojourn on earth.'[5]

Anne, like Agnes, was twenty when she embarked upon her second governess-ship, and although just half the seventy mile distance referred to above, Thorp Green Hall near York was the farthest from Haworth that Anne had ever travelled up to that point. The Murray family that Agnes encounters at Horton Lodge are clearly based this time upon the Robinsons, and whilst Agnes is relieved to find that they are better educated than the Bloomfields had been, she finds fault with their attitude towards life and love.

The Murray girls are at an age when they are making their débuts in society, and their mother's number one priority is finding suitably elevated matches for their daughters. In this sense, we see Mrs Murray as a reflection of Anne's former employer, Mrs Robinson. Lydia had arranged, for example, for her daughter Elizabeth, known as Bessie, to marry a wealthy man from a good family called Mr Milnes, but Anne gave her advice similar to that which Agnes gives Rosalie when a marriage to Sir Thomas Ashby, a man she cares nothing for, is proposed:

'It seemed a horrible thing to hurry on the inauspicious match, and not to give the poor creature time to think and reason on the irrevocable step she was about to take... I was amazed and horrified at Mrs Murray's heartlessness, or want of thought for the real good of her child; and, by my unheeded warnings and exhortations, I vainly strove to remedy the evil.'[6]

In the novel, Agnes' words are in vain, and Rosalie makes an unhappy marriage to Sir Thomas, but we have evidence that Anne's exhortations to Bessie Robinson were far from unheeded. In a letter dated 28th July 1848, Charlotte Brontë tells Ellen of the continued closeness of Anne to the charges she had left three years earlier:

'Anne continues to hear constantly, almost daily, from her old pupils, the Robinsons. They are now both engaged to different gentlemen – and if they do not change their minds – which they have already done two or three times – will probably be married in a few months. Not one spark of love does either of them profess for her future husband. One of them openly declares that interest alone guides her – and the other, poor thing! is acting according to her mother's wish, and is utterly indifferent herself to the man chosen for her... Anne does her best to cheer and counsel her – and she seems to cling to her quiet, former governess as her only friend.'[7]

Anne's counsel was listened to, and Bessie avoided the loveless match awaiting Rosalie Murray. Bessie Robinson's engagement to Mr Milnes was broken off, but the Milnes family contested the break and a court case and scandal ensued. Eventually Edmund and Lydia Robinson paid to the Milnes compensation of ninety pounds (a five figure sum in today's money), freeing Bessie from her obligations and allowing her to later enter into a happy marriage with William Jessop of Butterley Hall in Derbyshire.

In *Agnes Grey* the bonds between governess and charges remain intact after she leaves her position at Horton Lodge, and she is invited to stay at Ashby Park by Rosalie, now Lady Ashby. Here we learn that, just as Charlotte wrote of Bessie Robinson, Rosalie now looks upon her governess as her only true friend. Once again, Anne's first novel reflects the life she had lived, and as in the book, there was a further meeting between governess and her once pupils. In December 1848, two grand visitors arrived to see Anne. It was Bessie Robinson and Mary Clapham (née Robinson, and just married weeks earlier), and Charlotte described their visit:

'The Robinsons were here about a week ago – they are attractive and stylish looking girls – they seemed overjoyed to see Anne; when I went into the room they were cling-ing round her like two children – she, meantime, looking perfectly quiet and passive. Their manner evinced more levity and giddiness than pretension or pomposity.'[8]

These young women had travelled from Derbyshire to the snow-capped moors of Haworth to see their former governess one last time; it is clear how much they respect-ed and loved her, just as it is clear that much of *Agnes Grey* is based upon Anne's experiences in Mirfield and Thorp Green. Perhaps the most moving aspects of the novel, however, are when Anne writes about things she experienced purely in her imagination.

In the novel, Agnes falls in love with the assistant cu-rate, Edward Weston. Weston is a kind and caring man who takes great interest in his parishioners, so that we see him visiting the sick and elderly, reading to them and even rescuing a cat. At one point a Horton villager, in her Yorkshire accent, tells Agnes of his charitable deeds:

'About a three wik sin', when he seed how poor Jem shivered wi' cold, an' what pitiful fires we kept, he axed if wer stock of coals was nearly done. I telled him it was, an' we was ill set to get more: but you know, mum, I didn't think o' him helping us; but howsoever, he sent us a sack o' coals next day; an' we've had good fires ever sin: an' a great blessing it is, this winter time. But that's his way, Miss Grey: when he comes into a poor body's house a seein' sick folk, he like notices what they most stand I' need on; an' if he thinks they can't readily get it therseln, he never says nowt about it, but just gets it for 'em.'[9]

This passage is strongly reminiscent of a story Charlotte Brontë heard about William Weightman from a parish-ioner:

'Last Saturday night he [William Weightman] had been

sitting an hour in the parlour with Papa; and as he went away, I heard Papa say to him – "What is the matter with you? You seem in very low spirits tonight." "Oh, I don't know. I've been to see a poor young girl, who, I'm afraid, is dying." "Indeed, what is her name?" "Susan Bland, the daughter of John Bland, the superintendent." Now Susan Bland is my oldest and best scholar in the Sunday-school; and when I heard that, I thought I would go as soon as I could to see her. I did go, on Monday afternoon, and found her very ill and weak, and seemingly far on her way to that bourne whence no traveller returns. After sitting with her some time, I happened to ask her mother if she thought a little port wine would do her good. She replied that the doctor had recommended it, and that when Mr Weightman was last there, he had sent them a bottle of wine and a jar of preserves. She added, that he was always good-natured to poor folks, and seemed to have a deal of feeling and kind-heartedness about him.'[10]

There can be no doubt that Reverend Weston is at least in part a portrait of Reverend Weightman. It is Anne's greatest tribute to her lost love, but it is more than that too. Agnes leaves Horton Lodge and believes that she will never see Weston again, but at the climax of the book he returns and proposes to her. They marry and the book ends in a characteristically low-key, yet incredibly touching, finale:

'Our modest income is amply sufficient for our re-quirements: and by practising the economy we learned in harder times, and never attempting to imitate our richer neighbours, we manage not only to enjoy comfort and contentment ourselves, but to have every year something to lay by for our children, and something to give to those who need it. And now I think I have said sufficient.'[11]

A modest income and a modest ending to a modestly sized book, but in its modesty is its brilliance. Not a word is out of place, not an emotion overstated, and yet once read it lingers in your heart and mind. In it, Anne is finally giving herself, as Agnes, the dream ending that the reality of death had denied her; she could not marry William Weightman in life, but, shielded by the lapse of years and a few fictitious names as she had said in the opening paragraph, she will marry him on the page.

The nineteenth and twentieth century novelist George Moore, once painted by Edouard Manet, said: 'Agnes Grey is the most perfect prose narrative in English literature… a narrative simple and beautiful as a muslin dress… We know that we are reading a masterpiece. Nothing short of genius could have set them before us so plainly and yet with restraint… It is the one story in English literature in which style, characters and subject are in perfect keeping.'[12]

High praise for *Agnes Grey* indeed, and in my opinion fully deserved, but it came close to never being published at all. The sisters' first decision was to once more approach Aylott and Jones to see if their poetry publisher would publish their prose:

'C. E. & A. Bell are now preparing for the Press a work of fiction – consisting of three distinct and unconnected tales which may be published either together as a work of 3 vols. of the ordinary novel-size, or separately as single vols – as shall be deemed most advisable. It is not their intention to publish these tales on their own account.'[13]

Anne and her sisters were obviously confident in the quality of their work, there would be no paying for publication on this occasion. Months passed, however, and this initial confidence faded. Aylott and Jones wrote back to say that they did not publish prose fiction, and the sisters then entered upon the same pattern that their poetry submission had taken, receiving a succession of terse rejection notes or simply receiving the manuscripts back with no response at all. Their cause was not helped by the parcel being sent in the same packaging from one publisher to the next, with the name of the previous recipient crossed out. Their hopes of being published novelists seemed increasingly forlorn, but in the spring of 1847 everything changed.

A letter arrived to the Parsonage, addressed as always to Currer Bell Esq., from the publishing house of Thomas Cautley Newby of Cavendish Square, London. Newby offered to publish *Agnes Grey* and *Wuthering Heights*, but rejected *The Professor*. Further to this, he specified that Ellis and Acton Bell, as he thought them, would need to send him fifty pounds in advance to pay for the publication costs. This must have caused vigorous debate in the Parsonage; they had sworn that this time they would not pay to have their work published, but months of rejections with no encouragement had demonstrated how hard it would be to find a publisher on their terms. A further complication was that Charlotte, the elder sister who had driven the writing project forward, was now seemingly left out of it together. It must have been a heart-wrenching decision, one that Anne and Emily would have discussed as they walked the moors side by side, just as they had discussed everything together amidst the same stony paths and purple heather as children.

The decision was made to accept the terms, and the substantial sum of fifty pounds was sent. Anne and Emily had almost exhausted their aunt's inheritance; they were taking a real gamble, but if they did not take it, what was left for them? They had a dream and they knew the power of their work; they would follow their dream, come what may. Charlotte gave her sisters her support and her blessing; she rekindled her energies once more, and commenced work on another novel. If they did not want *The Professor* she would try something completely different, and, perhaps inspired by Anne's *Agnes Grey*, she had a tale about an English governess in mind.

Anne and Emily's novels were sent to Newby on 4th July 1847, and soon they were correcting and then submitting proofs. Excitement was mounting as they waited to receive their six author copies of their novels, but once again they were forced to wait, and wait. In fact, in the time between them submitting their corrected proofs and *Agnes Grey* and *Wuthering Heights* being published, Charlotte had completed her second novel, had it accepted and then printed, and under the guise of Currer Bell had become the toast of the literary scene and a best-selling author.

This second novel was, of course, *Jane Eyre*, and so impressed were the publishers Smith, Elder & Co that they expedited its publication allowing it to make its appearance in bookshops and circulating libraries in October 1847. The book and its author were an overnight success, and suddenly the name of Currer Bell was widely known, which did not escape the notice of Thomas Cautley Newby in Cavendish Square. Hoping to gain from the repute of Currer Bell, he finally published the works by Ellis and Acton Bell in December 1848, and he was careful that all advertising relating to their novels also mentioned Currer and *Jane Eyre*.

This was one of Newby's well-worn tricks, and indeed he had a repertoire of them so that he was part-publisher and part-con man. Anne and Emily had already fallen for one of his games, as he liked to sign up authors, make them pay an advance, and then publish them at some unspecified future date with little fanfare, if he published them at all. We shall soon see the repercussions of one of his other favourite stratagems: publishing books under names that made the public think they were by somebody else, and deliberately causing confusion about the identity of an author.

Despite this, the Brontës were not the only famous authors to enter his stable, and he was also the first person to publish a novel by Anthony Trollope.[14] He later capitalised on this, in characteristic fashion, by bringing out a series of novels by an in-house writer billed only as 'F. Trollope'. This was not, as readers were clearly led to believe, Anthony's mother, the popular novelist Fanny Trollope.

Newby's final trick in his repertoire was to release substandard sequels or prequels to books that were published by others, again in the hope that the public would believe they were the genuine article. He attempted to do this in 1859 by releasing a sequel to George Eliot's *Adam Bede*, but Eliot, real name Mary Anne Evans, heard of his plans and wrote to the Evening Mail denouncing him. We have Newby's typically slippery response, and it is of great interest to us for his passing comment on Anne Brontë:

'Sir – my attention has just been called to a letter in your paper to-day, signed "George Eliot", which charges me, untruly, with asserting and desiring to have it thought that *Adam Bede, Jun., a Sequel*, is the work of the individual bearing that name. My announcement contains no such suggestion, nor have I wished that "George Eliot" should be supposed to be the author of the work. With respect to "George Eliot's" allusion to the Life of Miss Brontë, the misrepresentation made there was quite as great as some others in the same work which became more notorious. I published all the novels of Acton and Ellis Bell. No disagreement ever took place between those ladies and me, and long after the publication of Jane Eyre, Miss Anne Brontë brought me a work, *The Tenant of Wildfell Hall*, which I published in due course. If "George Eliot" had confined himself to describing truly the terms of of my announcement of *Adam Bede, Jun., a Sequel*, he would neither have required to trouble you with a protest against what never happened, nor to reproduce a most palpable misrepresentation levelled at a publisher whose name the author of Miss Brontë's life [Elizabeth Gaskell] declined to give, but whom "George Eliot" for the first time identifies with me. I am, Sir, your obedient servant, Thomas Cautley Newby, 30, Welbeck-Street, Cavendish-square.'[15]

Of course, his suggestion had indeed been that *Adam Bede, Jun.* was by George Eliot, but following her intervention the sham novel was never released. It is fascinating, however, that Newby claims that Anne Brontë had no disagreement with him, and was so pleased with him that she wanted to have her second novel published by him too. This is a strange claim, given his treatment of her, but we shall look at it, and Anne's second novel, in the next chapter. Anne and Emily, like so many other Newby authors, received no money from him for their novels published in 1847. He was a publisher of no scruples, who used the Brontës like he used so many others, but on the other hand he was the only publisher who had shown any interest in Anne and Emily's novels, and the list they were working down was becoming depleted along with their hopes. Without Newby, for all his tricks, it is likely that there would be none of the Brontë novels we love today. 1847 ended with Anne, Charlotte and Emily all in print, but the year to come was to bring great triumphs and great tragedies.

8: The Upward Path

'BELIEVE NOT THOSE who say
The upward path is smooth,
Lest thou shouldst stumble in the way
And faint before the truth.

It is the only road
Unto the realms of joy;
But he who seeks that blest abode
Must all his powers employ.

Bright hopes and pure delights
Upon his course may beam,
And there amid the sternest heights,
The sweetest flowerets gleam; –

On all her breezes borne
Earth yields no scents like those;
But he, that dares not grasp the thorn
Should never crave the rose.

Arm, arm thee for the fight!
Cast useless loads away:
Watch through the darkest hours of night;
Toil through the hottest day.

Crush pride into the dust,
Or thou must needs be slack;
And trample down rebellious lust,
Or it will hold thee back.

Seek not thy treasure here;
Waive pleasure and renown;
The World's dread scoff undaunted bear,
And face its deadliest frown.

To labour and to love,
To pardon and endure,
To lift thy heart to God above,
And keep thy conscience pure, –
Be this thy constant aim,
Thy hope and thy delight, –
What matters who should whisper blame,
Or who should scorn or slight?
What matters – if thy God approve,
And if within thy breast,
Thou feel the comfort of his love,
The earnest of his rest?'

('The Narrow Way', dated 24th April 1848)

Upon receiving their author copies of *Agnes Grey* and *Wuthering Heights*, Anne and Emily were dismayed to find that errors they had corrected in the proofs were still present in the published volumes. Despite this the Bell novels gained positive reviews although some critics, linking these two novels to Charlotte's *Jane Eyre* declared the books too coarse for their liking. Typical of contemporary reviews was this one found in 'The Atlas':

'*Agnes Grey* is more level and more sunny [than *Wuthering Heights*]. Perhaps we shall best describe it as a somewhat coarse imitation of one of Miss Austin's [sic] charming stories... The story, though lacking the power and originality of *Wuthering Heights*, is infinitely more agreeable. It leaves no painful impression on the mind – some may think it leaves no impression at all.'[1]

The review in 'Douglas Jerrold's Weekly Newspaper' was much more positive, although on this occasion Anne's work was compared unfavourably to that of her sister rather than Jane Austen:

'We do not actually assert that the author must have been a governess himself, to describe as he does the minute torments and incessant tediums of her life, but he must have bribed some governess very largely, either with love or money, to reveal to him the secrets of her prison-house, or, he must have devoted extraordinary powers of observation and discovery to the elucidation of the subject. In either case, *Agnes Grey* is a tale well worth the writing and the reading. The heroine is a sort of younger sister to Jane Eyre, but inferior to her in every way.'[2]

As we shall see, Anne was not one to take unfair criticism lying down, and her poem 'The Narrow Way', as well as being a wonderful hymn is also in part her assertion that she will carry on regardless of scorn and slights from critics. Criticism galvanised Anne, but it had a dispiriting effect upon Emily. Her novel *Wuthering Heights* was a work of towering genius, and yet critics had failed to appreciate it. Whilst there is a letter from Newby referring to the possibility of Emily writing a second novel for him, there is no evidence that she had commenced writing it, or had seriously considered doing so. It is possible, even likely, that, even if fate had not intervened a year later, this masterful novelist would never have written a prose work again.

Anne, on the other hand, was determined to write on, and to use her talents to examine some of the darker elements of life in early Victorian England. Her second novel *The Tenant of Wildfell Hall* did just that, and in her preface to the second edition, in response to critics of both this book and *Agnes Grey*, Anne explained her reasons for writing it and her view on what the aim of writing itself should always be:

'My object in writing the following pages was not simply to amuse the Reader, neither was it to gratify my own taste, nor yet to ingratiate myself with the Press and the Public: I wished to tell the truth, for truth always conveys its own moral to those who are able to receive it. But as the priceless treasure too frequently hides at the bottom of a well, it needs some courage to dive for it, especially as he that does so will be likely to incur more scorn and obloquy for the mud and water into which he has ventured to plunge, than thanks for the jewel he procures; as, in like manner, she who undertakes the cleansing of a careless bachelor's apartment will be liable to more abuse for the dust she raises than commendation for the clearance she effects. Let it not be imagined, however, that I consider myself competent to reform the errors and abuses of society, but only that I would fain contribute my humble quota towards so good an aim, and if I can gain the public ear at all, I would rather whisper a few wholesome truths therein than much soft nonsense... I love to give innocent pleasure. Yet, be it understood, I shall not limit my ambition to this or even to producing a perfect work of art: time and talents so spent, I should consider wasted and mis-applied. Such humble talents as God has given me I will endeavour to put to their greatest use; if I am able to amuse, I will try to benefit too; and when I feel it my duty to speak an unpalatable truth, with the help of God, I will speak it, though it be to the prejudice of my name and to the detriment of my reader's immediate pleasure as well as my own.'[3]

Anne was still reeling from her time at Thorp Green Hall when she wrote about Wildfell Hall and those 'undreamt of experiences of human nature'[4] helped to inform and populate her second novel, which was published in

June 1848, just six months after *Agnes Grey*. As the book opens, the titular heroine is a mysterious woman who has moved into Wildfell Hall with her child, and who is apparently making a living as an artist. As a single mother, Helen Graham (eventually revealed as an assumed name), arouses the suspicion of villagers but a local farmer, Gilbert Markham, falls in love with her.

Gilbert's family are appalled at his growing closeness to Helen, especially as they frown upon her actions such as preventing her five-year-old son Arthur from drinking alcohol. Gossip also rages about the likeness of young Arthur to Frederick Lawrence, Gilbert's friend and the landlord of Wildfell Hall. After seeing Helen and Frederick seemingly in a tryst, Gilbert flies into a rage and he later knocks Frederick off his horse, nearly killing him. Helen then gives Gilbert her diary, and her true, terrible story is revealed.

Frederick, we learn, is the brother of Helen and she has taken refuge at Wildfell Hall after fleeing with her child from her drunk and abusive husband, Arthur Huntingdon. In this incredibly powerful and frank section of her book, Anne shows in graphic detail how a narcissistic husband can degrade his wife, using their own child as a weapon against her, before finally falling victim to his own weakness and addictions. Under the laws of the day, Helen was in effect her husband's property and divorce was virtually impossible; she is a prisoner at Huntingdon's Grassdale Manor as year after year her husband's behaviour becomes more extreme. We see riotous drink and drug-fuelled parties, wives being beaten by their husbands, and marital infidelity – if *Agnes Grey* had Jane Austen-like qualities, we are far from Austen territory here.

Eventually, after an earlier attempt was thwarted, Helen

escapes from Grassdale, but she returns voluntarily after learning that her husband is dying as a result of his excesses. She tries to make him repent and turn to God, but even this is in vain. The tyrant is dead, and Anne closes this brutally unflinching book with a happy ending as the now free Helen marries Gilbert.

This is a Brontë book like no other, and readers today are often shocked to find it so modern in its outlook, and so unafraid to tackle difficult subjects. It has been called one of the first fully formed works of feminist fiction, and a book that places Anne 'in the forefront of feminist thought in the nineteenth century.'[5] May Sinclair, the novelist and suffragette, wrote in a 1914 introduction to Anne's work that, 'the slamming of Helen Huntingdon's bedroom door against her husband reverberated through Victorian England.'[6]

At the start of the novel's thirty-fourth chapter, Helen finally reveals her true thoughts, to herself and the reader, about the man who has mistreated her, cheated on her, and is striving to influence her child for the bad:

'Oh! When I think how fondly, how foolishly I have loved him, how madly I have trusted him, how constantly I have laboured, and studied, and prayed, and struggled for his advantage; and how cruelly he has trampled on my love, betrayed my trust, scorned my prayers and tears, and efforts for his preservation – crushed my hopes, destroyed my youth's best feelings, and doomed me to a life of hopeless misery – as far as man can do it – it is not enough to say that I no longer love my husband – I HATE him! The word stares me in the face like a guilty confession, but it is true: I hate him – I hate him!'[7]

By leaving her husband, Helen breaks the antiquated marital laws of the time; her husband has her possessions, but he cannot have her body and he cannot have her mind. It was a courageous move in a courageous book, and as May Sinclair intimated, it has served as a rallying cry to women in similar situations throughout the nineteenth century and beyond.

This is an undoubted masterpiece of Victorian fiction, one in which Anne shows the power of her imagination and the brilliance of her writing, but as in *Agnes Grey* before it, Anne also uses stories and people that she knew from her own personal experience. Some claim that Helen is based upon Annabella Milbanke, the wronged wife of Lord Byron, but whilst Arthur's excesses are Byronic we can look a little closer to home to find the real inspiration for Helen.

The stories told by the beloved Parsonage servant Tabby Aykroyd have often, rightly, been credited for influencing the Brontë's work, but Anne was clearly enchanted by the stories her aunt told her too. She obviously knew the sad tale of her Aunt Jane, older sister to Maria and Elizabeth, who in Penzance married a Methodist priest named Reverend John Kingston, and its influence can be seen in Anne's second novel.

Six years after their marriage John Kingston was suddenly defrocked and thrown out of the Methodist church, and we now know that he had been convicted by his peers of theft and of having sex with two men. Faced with shame in England, in 1808 John, along with his pregnant and far from happy wife and three children, emigrated to start a new life in Baltimore, America. The marriage must have deteriorated still further, for in 1809 Jane left America and returned to her family in Penzance. With her was her baby daughter Eliza, who had been born in America, but she had to leave her three older children behind with their father. Once back in Penzance, her sister Elizabeth provided Jane with enough money to start a business, and she later left her niece Eliza an equal share in her will alongside Anne, Charlotte and Emily.[8]

Here then we have a Brontë aunt who was a single mother who had fled an unhappy marriage, taking her young child with her, and who was then supported by her sibling. Aunt Jane was surely therefore the prototype of Helen, the tenant of Wildfell Hall.

There has long also been suspicion that the alcoholic hedonist, Arthur Huntingdon, was a veiled portrait of Anne's brother Branwell, but whilst Branwell's addiction was reaching its zenith at the time Anne wrote her book she still loved him dearly, and for all his challenges he was never the cruel villain that Huntingdon was. Even so, it may be that Charlotte Brontë saw Huntingdon as a portrait of her brother, and was upset that his weaknesses were being shown to the reading world. Could this be the reason that she gave her famously damning verdict on *The Tenant of Wildfell Hall*?:

'"Wildfell Hall" it hardly appears desirable to preserve. The choice of subject in that work is a mistake – it was too little consonant with the character, tastes, and ideas of the gentle, retiring, inexperienced writer. She wrote it under a strange, conscientious, half-ascetic notion of accomplishing a painful penance and a severe duty.'[9]

The novel was also roundly attacked by critics of the day, with one lamenting its 'scandalous insistence on present-ing scenes which public decency usually forbids.',[10] and *The Rambler* warning its readers that, 'the scenes which the heroine relates in her diary are of the most disgusting and revolting species.'[11]

The reading public were thus warned about the

scandalous nature of Anne's book, and this had two effects. Firstly, Anne felt compelled to strike back at these critics in her preface to the second edition looked at earlier in the chapter, in which she said:

'When we have to do with vice and vicious characters, I maintain it is better to depict them as they really are than as they would wish to appear. To represent a bad thing in its least offensive light is, doubtless, the most agreeable course for a writer of fiction to pursue; but is it the most honest, or the safest? Is it better to reveal the snares and pitfalls of life to the young and thoughtless traveller, or to cover them with branches and flowers? O Reader! if there were less of this delicate concealment of facts this whispering, 'Peace, peace' when there is no peace, there would be less of sin and misery to the young of both sexes who are left to wring their bitter knowledge from experience.'[12]

The second effect of the critics' warning was that the public immediately went out and purchased *The Tenant of Wildfell Hall* in large numbers, so that it sold even faster than *Jane Eyre* had done. Anne suddenly had a huge success on her hands, but that brought with it an unexpected chain of events leading to tragedy.

Anne's publisher Thomas Cautley Newby, ever alert to an opportunity to boost sales by twisting the truth a little (or a lot), told an American publisher called Harper & Brothers that *The Tenant of Wildfell Hall* was by the same author as *Jane Eyre* and that Currer, Acton and Ellis Bell were in fact one and the same person. Unbeknownst to Newby, Harper already had a deal in place with Smith, Elder & Co, the London based publishers of *Jane Eyre*, for first option on American rights to any new books by Currer Bell, so he wrote to George Smith for clarification. Smith was equally puzzled and he in turn wrote to his author, Currer Bell, in Haworth. It was a letter that changed literary history, for better and worse.

The letter arrived in Haworth on the morning of 7th July 1848, and its message fell like a hammer blow upon the three sisters who read it. They had preserved their anonymity through the use of pen names, but this precaution had now led to Charlotte's publisher asking her to clear her name against allegations of dishonesty. Honesty was everything to the sisters, but revealing the truth would take a big step and a long journey. Sending a letter would be pointless, the only way they could prove that Currer, Acton and Ellis were separate people would be to throw off their masks and admit their real identities.

Emily, even now, refused to lay down her Ellis Bell mask, but she also stated that as the letter concerned Anne and Charlotte alone she would give them their blessing if they wanted to reveal their true selves. It says a lot for the anguish the letter caused Anne and Charlotte that they had packed their bags, gathered together money, and were on a train from Leeds to London by eight o'clock on the evening of the letter's arrival.

After an overnight journey, the train arrived at Euston station at 4.30 in the morning. Stepping down from the train, even at this early hour, Anne must have been in awe of the sights, sounds and smells around her. This was to be the only journey she ever made beyond the boundaries of Yorkshire, and it was a magical one. A cab was hailed that conveyed the sisters to the only place Charlotte knew in London, the Chapter Coffee House on Paternoster Row, in the shadow of St. Paul's Cathedral, where she, Emily and her father had stayed en route to Brussels six years earlier.

Heavy rain created a gloomy aspect to this early morning in the city, and travel and the stress of the letter had brought on one of the headaches from which Charlotte frequently suffered. Nevertheless, they wasted no time and, once the morning had begun in earnest, they set out for the offices of Smith, Elder & Co at 65 Cornhill.

With what trepidation must Anne and Charlotte have pushed open the door and entered the bookshop situated below the publisher's offices? They could have turned round, headed to Euston and travelled back to the safety of their parsonage two hundred miles away but, no, they had come a long way for a very definite purpose, there was no turning back now.

Naive to the ways of business it had not occurred to the sisters that a businessman may be absent from his office on this, a Saturday morning, but as it happened George Smith, a wealthy young man who had recently inherited the business, was a workaholic and already behind his desk. He later recounted what happened on that unique day:

'That particular Saturday morning I was at work in my room, when a clerk reported that two ladies wished to see me. I was very busy and sent out to ask their names. The clerk returned to say that the ladies declined to give their names, but wished to see me on a private matter. After a moment's hesitation I told him to show them in. I was in the midst of my correspondence, and my thoughts were far away from 'Currer Bell' and 'Jane Eyre.' Two rather quaintly dressed little ladies, pale-faced and anxious-looking, walked into my room; one of them came forward and presented me with a letter addressed, in my own handwriting, to "Currer Bell, Esq." I noticed that the letter had been opened, and said, with some sharpness, "Where did you get this from?" "From the post-office" was the reply; "it was addressed to me. We have both come that you might have ocular proof that there are at least two of us."

This then was Currer Bell in person. I need hardly say that I was at once keenly interested, not to say excited.'[13]

The brilliant Currer Bell and the fierce Acton Bell, writer of that season's scandalous hit novel, were standing before him in the diminutive forms of Charlotte and Anne Brontë; it was not what George Smith had expected, but he was no less delighted for that. He invited his colleague, W. S. Williams, to his office to meet them and Williams too was amazed at what he saw; it was he who first read the manuscript of *Jane Eyre* and recognised its genius, and after this meeting he and Charlotte became friends and regular correspondents.

Smith too became a close friend of Charlotte in subsequent years, and he even travelled on holiday to Scotland with her, although he famously gave his verdict that, 'she would have given all her genius and her fame to have been beautiful. Perhaps few women ever existed more anxious to be pretty than she, or more angrily conscious of the circumstance that she was not pretty.'[14]

He was more complimentary about Anne's looks, and it is from him that we have the only description of her adult appearance:

'This is the only occasion on which I saw Anne Brontë. She was a gentle, quiet, rather subdued person, by no means pretty, yet of a pleasing appearance. Her manner was curiously expressive of a wish for protection and encouragement, a kind of constant appeal which invited sympathy.'[15]

Anne and Charlotte had planned on meeting Smith, proving their innocence of any charges of dishonesty implied by the letter, and then returning home as soon as possible, but at Smith's insistence they remained in London for four days. During that time he and Williams showed the Brontës some of the delights on offer in the capital, including a visit to the galleries of the Royal Academy and a walk through Kensington Gardens. The sisters also enjoyed lunch at the Williams household, where Charlotte and Anne listened to one of his eight daughters sing a duet with another guest, the daughter of John Keats' great friend, Leigh Hunt.

Two events in this London sojourn particularly thrilled Anne. On Saturday evening she and Charlotte were accompanied by George Smith and his sister to the grand Royal Italian Opera in Covent Garden, on the site of what is now the Royal Opera House. Rossini's musical masterpiece 'The Barber of Seville' was being performed, and although 'Anne was calm and gentle, as she always is',[16] the evening must have been a sheer delight for her. Anne Brontë was a great lover of music, and she amassed a substantial collection of sheet music, particularly favouring light operatic pieces by the likes of Rossini.

Anne and Emily were also accomplished pianists, thanks to an upright piano which their father Patrick had bought for the Parsonage in 1834. We have Ellen Nussey's description of their musicality:

'A little later on, there was the addition of a piano. Emily, after some application, played with precision and brilliancy. Anne played also, but she preferred soft harmonies and vocal music. She sang a little; her voice was weak, but very sweet in tone.'[17]

Anne's passion for music meant that Smith's operatic treat for her was inspired, and she must also have loved her visit to St. Stephen's Church in Walbrook on Sunday morning, accompanied by Charlotte, W. S. Williams and his family. Despite being able to see the mighty St. Paul's from their lodgings at the coffee house, Anne wanted to attend the service at St. Stephen's instead as she knew of the glowing reputation of its preacher, George Croly. Unfortunately, Reverend Croly was not preaching on that Sunday, but Anne would still have been impressed by the majestic interior of what is still one of London's most beautiful churches.

There is no record of whether Anne and Charlotte also visited the offices of Newby during their days in London, or whether they left that in the hands of Charlotte's altogether more reliable publisher. Despite his version of events in the *Evening Mail* we can be sure that Anne would not have been happy with Newby's methods, and it seems impossible that she would have chosen him as a publisher for any further novels after *The Tenant of Wildfell Hall*. It was Smith who published posthumous editions of Anne and Emily's works, presumably having bought the rights from Thomas Newby.

Anne and Charlotte returned to Haworth on Tuesday 11th July, 1848. They were exhausted but elated; laden with books, a parting gift from George Smith, they had proved their honesty and enjoyed four days in which they experienced the very best that London high society could provide. Surely now they could look forward to a bright future where their genius would be recognised and rewarded? Little did they know that within a year of that triumphant homecoming three members of this close-knit family group would be dead.

9: A Dreadful Darkness

'A DREADFUL DARKNESS closes in
On my bewildered mind;
O let me suffer and not sin,
Be tortured yet resigned.
Through all this world of whelming mist
Still let me look to Thee,
And give me courage to resist
The Tempter till he flee.
Weary I am – O give me strength
And leave me not to faint;
Say Thou wilt comfort me at length
And pity my complaint.
I've begged to serve Thee heart and soul,
To sacrifice to Thee
No niggard portion, but the whole
Of my identity.
I hoped amid the brave and strong
My portioned task might lie,
To toil amid the labouring throng
With purpose pure and high.
But Thou hast fixed another part,
And Thou hast fixed it well;
I said so with my breaking heart
When first the anguish fell.
For Thou hast taken my delight
And hope of life away,
And bid me watch the painful night
And wait the weary day.

The hope and the delight were Thine;
I bless Thee for their loan;
I gave Thee while I deemed them mine
Too little thanks, I own.
Shall I with joy Thy blessings share
And not endure their loss?
Or hope the martyr's crown to wear
And cast away the cross?'

(The opening of 'Last Lines', written 7th January 1849)

Following Anne's return to the Parsonage from London she commenced work on a preface to a second edition of *The Tenant of Wildfell Hall*. So quickly had her novel sold that the first edition had sold out in a month, but this afforded Anne an opportunity to respond to her critics and to set out a manifesto for what she saw as the most important element in writing: truth. She also addressed another matter of great concern to her: the right of women to read and write whatever men could, and to be judged in the same way for doing so:

'Respecting the author's identity, I would have it to be distinctly understood that Acton Bell is neither Currer nor Ellis Bell, and therefore let not his faults be attributed to them. As to whether the name be real or fictitious, it cannot greatly signify to those who know him only by his works. As little, I should think, can it matter whether the writer so designated is a man, or a woman, as one or two of my critics profess to have discovered. I take the imputation in good part, as a compliment to the just delineation of my female characters; and though I am bound to attribute much of the severity of my censors to this suspicion, I make no effort to refute it, because, in my

125

own mind, I am satisfied that if a book is a good one, it is so whatever the sex of the author may be. All novels are, or should be, written for both men and women to read, and I am at a loss to conceive how a man should permit himself to write anything that would be really disgraceful to a woman, or why a woman should be censured for writing anything that would be proper and becoming for a man.'[1]

This is clearly in response to Newby's assertion that the Bells were one person, and to anyone who may have had similar ideas. Anne Brontë had a quiet voice and was a naturally shy person, but she shows here that she was unafraid to speak up for what she believed in. We see it in this preface, in her life and in her work, which is why she is in many ways the most radical and powerful of the Brontë sisters. The commercial success of her second novel had helped to empower Anne so that she now felt able to make this forthright pronouncement at the beginning of the second edition of her second novel, and that self-confidence would surely have served her well in a writing career to come. Unbeknownst to Anne and her family, time was running out.

Although a severe winter cold had affected all of the family at the start of 1848, Anne, Charlotte and Emily had all been in good health at the time of Anne's London journey in July. Branwell's dependency upon alcohol and opium had been growing in recent years, and his behaviour could often be erratic, but he himself had predicted that, against his own wishes, his robust nature would see him endure a long life.

Shortly after Anne's return from London, however, her brother's condition rapidly deteriorated, and he was soon bed-bound, his wasted frame testimony to the effects that his excesses were having upon him, or so people thought. Anne and Emily took on the role of nursemaids, the close relationship that Branwell and Charlotte had once enjoyed having long since evaporated, as they had done so often before, most famously on the occasion when they found that Branwell had fallen asleep whilst trying to read by candlelight and set his bedroom on fire. They doused the flames and rescued their brother, and they must have wondered then how many such episodes they would have to witness in future.[2]

The summer of 1848 saw Branwell's final repose however, and this time it was not a drink-induced malady that he could eventually shake off. On 24th September 1848, the bedridden and increasingly thin Branwell was visited by his great friend John Brown, the sexton who was preparing to make the short journey to the church to ring its bells. As he turned round, Branwell cried out, 'John, I'm dying!'[3] Branwell's father and sisters were called, and all were amazed to hear him give a final 'amen' to his father's fervent prayers. With the last reserves of his strength he rose to his feet, embraced Patrick, and died.

Anne remembered the love she had shared with her only brother, especially in her childhood when he had guided her way and had drawn pictures to entertain her. In recent years his health and behaviour had deteriorated as his addictions had grown, but in today's society the likelihood is that he would be diagnosed with mental health problems and given the appropriate help. Branwell's life and character was summed up well by his friend Francis Grundy:

'His letters to me revealed more of his soul's struggles than probably was known to any other. Branwell Brontë was no domestic demon – he was just a man moving in a mist, who lost his way.'[4]

It was a keenly felt loss for Anne, but an even greater one followed on its heels. Branwell's wasted frame had not long been interred in the Brontë family vault when it became apparent that Emily too was seriously ill and becoming weaker by the day. Anne begged her beloved sister to seek medical help and to try the remedies that were being suggested to her, but Emily, echoing the 'old stoic' in one of her own poems, refused any assistance at all. Always in love with nature, and the cycle of life and death that she saw acted out around her, Emily would let nature take its course – as in the last line of that poem, she would have 'courage to endure.'[5]

Homeopathic medicine, very popular at the time, was suggested by Charlotte's now regular correspondent W. S. Williams, but Emily dismissed it out of hand as 'quackery'.[6] By late November, Emily's condition had deteriorated still further, leaving Charlotte to write despairingly to Ellen Nussey:

'I told you Emily was ill in my last letter – she has not rallied yet – she is very ill: I believe if you were to see her your impression would be that there is no hope: a more hollow, wasted pallid aspect I have not yet beheld. The deep tight cough continues; the breathing after the least exertion is a rapid pant – and their symptoms are accompanied by pain in the chest and side... In this state, she resolutely refuses to see a doctor; she will give no explanation of her feelings, she will scarcely allow her illness to be alluded to. Our position is, and has been for some weeks, exquisitely painful. God only knows how all this is to terminate. More than once I have been forced boldly to regard the terrible event of her loss as possible and even probable. But nature shrinks from such thoughts. I think Emily seems the nearest thing to my heart in this world.'[7]

As Christmas approached it became clear that Emily, aged just thirty, was entering her final days, but there was nothing that Anne could do for the woman who was like a twin to her other than hold her hand, comb her hair and say a prayer by her bedside as she listened to Emily's strained breathing. Even at this time, however, Anne could find some fleeting moments of happiness as it was in this month of trial that her former pupils, the Robinson girls, visited her – perhaps freed at last to visit her by the absence of Branwell. Ellen also observed a smile play briefly upon Anne's face when she too visited Haworth Parsonage in December 1848:

'I observed a slow smile spreading across Anne's face as she sat reading before the fire. I asked her why she was smiling, and she replied: "Only because I see they have inserted one of my poems."'[8]

Anne was the only Brontë sister to have her poetry published without having to pay for it, having had her poem 'The Three Guides' published in the prestigious Fraser's Magazine, and now, in their December edition, 'The Narrow Way.'

It was 'The Narrow Way' that caused Anne to smile even in this time of personal heartbreak for her, the poem which headed the previous chapter. It's a poem of defiance, a poem of strength in the face of adversity, and so in many ways it is the perfect poem to represent Anne herself. The opening stanza is now on a plaque inside the Old School Rooms in Haworth, a tribute to the woman who had served so well as a Sunday school teacher there.

On 19th December 1848, the moment that Anne had dreaded arrived. With Anne and Charlotte alongside her, Emily Brontë died in the Parsonage dining room. The couch on which she and Anne had so often sat composing verse, feeding their dogs and discussing Gondal, had the honour of holding the body of this great woman as she drew her final breath. It was a mournful Christmas period in the Parsonage, not least because Anne too was now showing similar symptoms to those Emily had demonstrated, as Charlotte disclosed in another bleak letter in this most terrible of times:

'I now look at Anne and wish she were well and strong – but she is neither.'[9]

By January 1849 Anne was finding breathing difficult, especially after any exertion, and when she drew her handkerchief from her mouth after a coughing fit it had the telltale flecks of blood upon it. A distraught Patrick arranged for Dr Thomas Pridgin Teale, a lung specialist from Leeds, to examine his youngest daughter, and the ever dependable Ellen was there to provide support, in more ways than one, to Anne and Charlotte. She described the outcome of the examination:

'Anne was looking sweetly pretty and flushed, and in capital spirits for an invalid. While consultations were going on in Mr Brontë's study, Anne was very lively in conversation, walking around the room supported by me. Mr Brontë joined us after Mr Teale's departure and, seating himself on the couch, he drew Anne towards him and said, "My dear little Anne." That was all – but it was understood.'[10]

The doctor had confirmed what they all, Anne included, knew – she had tuberculosis (known as consumption at the time) and there was no hope of recovery. It was tuberculosis that had claimed Emily's life in December and also tuberculosis that killed Branwell in September, his death coming not as a result of his addictions. In a 1972 investigation into the Brontë deaths, Professor Philip

Rhodes pointed out that tuberculosis was not one of the major killers in Haworth, but was instead the terror of large, tightly packed urban areas, like London. The speed with which tuberculosis devastated the Parsonage after Anne and Charlotte's return from the capital in July 1848 suggests that one of them had been exposed to tubercular bacilli there and brought them north to the Parsonage.[11]

This sentence of death weighed heavily upon Anne who could feel herself growing weaker by the day. It is under this heaviest of oppressions that she wrote the opening to an untitled poem, her final poetic work, which Charlotte later titled 'Last Lines'. The opening section which appears at the head of this chapter was dated by Anne on 7th January 1849, and we see the dreadful darkness closing in on her weary mind and body as she awaits her final day. The poem initially finished with Anne thinking of casting away the cross, but when we look at the manuscript today we find that exactly three weeks later Anne took up her pen once more.

Anne added seven further stanzas, her real 'last lines' when it came to poetry, and concluded them with the date of 28th January 1849, and in these verses we see a change in her mood. She now vows to meet every blow with patience, and to gather fortitude with pain, before giving the poem its new and definitive ending:

'Should death be standing at the gate
Thus should I keep my vow;
But, Lord, whate'er my future fate
So let me serve thee now.'[12]

The three weeks between the composition of the two distinct sections of the poem were ones of intense turmoil for Anne. Would she sink beneath the weight of her grief for her siblings and herself, or find strength from her faith and face whatever awaited her head on? Anne was small in stature (around five feet tall) and quiet in voice, but she showed here, as so often throughout her life, that she possessed huge inner strength. She would not go gently into the night, but would instead fight to live for as long as she could.

Unlike Emily before her, Anne took all the medicine that was offered to her, but eventually found that the oleaginous medicine was making her so sick that she could no longer take it. She also used a respirator on a daily basis, kindly supplied by Ellen. Anne, and all around her, knew that the consumption could not be defeated, but she hoped to slow its progress and live for a few more weeks, months, maybe even years. With this in mind, Anne's thoughts turned once more to the place she loved – Scarborough.

One reason that Scarborough became so popular in the nineteenth century was its large spa that was said to contain naturally healing waters. During her summers visiting the resort with the Robinson family, Anne frequented the spa on many occasions and she often heard reports of miraculous recoveries attributed to its powers.

Anne now put the case for a journey to Scarborough, but Charlotte, realising how weak her sister was and fearful that she would not survive the journey there, tried to persuade her to wait until the warmer summer months arrived. Always astute, Anne realised that she needed an ally on board if she was to persuade Charlotte to let her travel, and so she wrote to Ellen Nussey on 5th April 1849. It is a masterful letter from one so ill at the time of its writing; the paper is bordered in black to show that its writer is in mourning, for Emily, and it is written cross-style, that is with sentences written first vertically then horizontally, so that the page has to be turned to read the whole. It was a common practice in order to save paper at the time, but it seems a strange economy given Anne's parlous state. The following extracts reveal the purpose of the letter, her plans for one final journey to Scarborough, and her attitude to life and death:

'I do not think there would be any great responsibility in the matter. I know, and every body knows that you would be as kind and helpful as any one could possibly be, and I hope I should not be very troublesome. It would be as a companion not as a nurse that I should wish for your company, otherwise I should not venture to ask it. As for your kind and often repeated invitation to Brookroyd, pray give my sincere thanks to your mother and sisters, but tell them I could not think of inflicting my presence upon them as I now am. It is very kind of them to make so light of the trouble but trouble there must be, more or less – and certainly no pleasure from the society of a silent invalid stranger – I hope however that Charlotte will by some means make it possible to accompany me after all, for she is certainly very delicate and greatly needs a change of air and scene to renovate her constitution. And then your going with me before the end of May is apparently out of the question, unless you are disappointed in your visitors, but I should be reluctant to wait till then if the weather would at all permit an earlier departure. You say May is a trying month and so say others… the doctors say that change of air or removal to a better climate would hardly ever fail of success in consumptive cases if the remedy were taken in time, but the reason why there are so many disappointments is, that it is generally deferred till it is too late. Now I would not commit this error; and to say the truth, though I suffer much less from pain and fever than I did when you were with us, I am decidedly weaker and very much thinner, my cough still troubles me a good deal, especially in the night, and, what seems worse than all I am subject to great shortness of breath on going up stairs or any slight exertion. Under these circumstances I think there is no time to be lost. I have no horror of death: if I thought it inevitable I think I could quietly resign myself to the prospect, in the hope that you, dear Miss Nussey, would give as much of your company as you possibly could to Charlotte and be a sister to her in my stead. But I wish it would please God to spare me not only for Papa's and Charlotte's sakes, but because I long to do some good in the world before I leave it. I have many schemes in my head for future practise – humble and limited indeed – but still I should not like them to come to nothing, and myself to have lived to so little purpose. But God's will be done.'[13]

Ellen fought Anne's cause, and eventually Charlotte had to admit that the journey, Anne's final wish, could not be delayed any longer. On 24th May, Ellen arrived at Haworth Parsonage. She had not seen Anne since the day of her diagnosis six months earlier, as Dr. Teale had ordered Ellen to return to her home at Birstall lest she too should be exposed to the disease. Charlotte had warned Ellen to expect a great change in Anne:

'She is very much emaciated, far worse than when you were with us; her arms are no thicker than a little child's. The least exertion brings a shortness of breath. She goes out a little every day, but we creep rather than walk.'[14]

The 24th May was a Thursday. It was the day that Anne, Charlotte and Ellen commenced their journey to

Scarborough. It was the last day that Patrick would see his youngest daughter and hold her hand.

To break the journey, the three women stayed in York overnight at the George Hotel on Coney Street – a Waterstones bookshop now occupies the building. Ellen kept a detailed record of this journey, and we know that in York Anne purchased bonnets and ribbons so that they could look their best in Scarborough. They were to stay at number 2 The Cliff, part of the Wood's Lodgings complex that Anne had stayed in with the Robinsons. Then she was a servant, now she was the woman of importance; she was able to pay for the luxurious accommodation as just three months earlier she had been left two hundred pounds in the Will of her godmother, Fanny Outhwaite. This choice of accommodation was decided upon despite the offer of the free use of a house that Margaret Wooler now owned in Scarborough, but her property overlooked the North Bay rather than the South Bay that Anne particularly loved.

It is also from Ellen that we learn how in York Anne asked to be taken to the majestic York Minster, and how she was wheeled there in a bath chair they had hired. The Minster is the largest Gothic cathedral in Northern Europe, magnificent inside and out. For a long time, Anne sat silently at the back of the cathedral, looking up at its towering roof, ornate carvings and stained glass, until she exclaimed:

'If finite power can do this, what is the...'[15]

Her sentence remained half-finished, and Charlotte wheeled her out of the Minster, worried that she was becoming overwrought with emotion from pondering on the infinite power awaiting her.

On 25th May, they arrived by train in Scarborough,

where they made a purchase of dandelion coffee as well as tickets that allowed them unlimited access to the spa and to the grand bridge that connected it to Wood's Lodgings.

Over the next two days, Anne once more enjoyed the sights and sounds of Scarborough that she had encountered so many times before. She even took a donkey ride along the South Bay beach, conveyed by a cart pulled behind it. Anne insisted on taking the reins herself, as she didn't want the driver to whip the animal. Ellen and Charlotte were left behind to watch her trundle further down the sands; it was a solitary moment for Anne, who had a lot to think about but little time in which to do it.

We know also that Anne insisted on attending the spa on her own, taking the waters surrounded by the ghosts of Scarborough summers past. She walked slowly back to her accommodation but faltered and then fell to the floor and had to be carried indoors by the hired servant, Jane Jefferson.

On Sunday Anne asked if Charlotte and Ellen could take her to a church, but an emotional Charlotte explained that Anne was too ill to go. Realising that the end was approaching Anne then asked her sister if she thought they should return to Haworth, but it was too late for that also.

On the morning of the 28th May, a Monday, Ellen had to carry Anne downstairs so that she could sit by the window. Passing down the steps a jolt sent Anne's head lolling forward into Ellen's, who feared immediately that her friend was dead, but Anne looked up and apologised for the inconvenience she was causing.

A doctor was called to the room, and he pronounced the judgement that Anne had undergone 'the change';

she was entering her final hours on earth. Anne was now bathed in calm resolution and she bade Charlotte and Ellen to care for each other like sisters in her absence. She continued to look out of the window, the only sounds being her laboured breathing, the ticking of a clock and the occasional sobs of her sister.

Anne faced her final hours without flinching. She saw the seagulls fly past her window, and looked down at the sea and the sands that she loved. The ebb and tide of the sea was never ending, and she was confident that her soul was just as eternal. Her faith was stronger than ever; perhaps her mind turned to a poem that she had composed four years earlier:

> 'I hear the great Redeemer say
> "Blessed are ye that mourn".
> Hold on thy course nor deem it strange
> That earthly cords are riven.
> Man may lament the wondrous change
> But "There is joy in Heaven"!'[16]

Perhaps too, as she looked down at the beach, she thought of the scene she herself had set there in her novel *Agnes Grey*. On these same sands Agnes and Weston are reunited; soon, she believed, she would surely be reunited with William Weightman:

'I walked, skipped, and stumbled back to the smooth, wide sands, and resolved to proceed to a certain bold projection in the cliffs, and then return. Presently, I heard a snuffling sound behind me, and then a dog came frisking and wriggling at my feet. It was my own Snap – the little, dark, wire-haired terrier! When I spoke his name, he leapt up in my face and yelled for joy. Almost as much delighted as himself, I caught the little creature in my arms, and kissed him repeatedly. But how had he come to be there? He could not have dropped from the sky, or come all that way alone; it must be either his master, the rat-catcher, or somebody else that had brought him; so, repressing my extravagant caresses, and endeavouring to repress his likewise, I looked round and beheld – Mr Weston!'[17]

Turning to her sister, Anne called out, 'Take courage, Charlotte, take courage'. A little after two o'clock Mrs Jefferson brought a meal and began to prepare the table. All was silent, the air was calm. So calm that she did not notice that Anne Brontë was dead.

The Search for Anne
Brontë's Last Words

FOLLOWING ANNE BRONTË's death, a deep depression fell again upon Charlotte, leaving the ever faithful and dependable Ellen to comfort Charlotte and arrange her departed friend's funeral and headstone at the same time. It is perhaps for this reason that a number of errors were initially made on the memorial that stands next to Anne's grave at St. Mary's churchyard, in the shadow of Scarborough Castle: the timeless building that Anne had earlier chosen as the setting for Weston's proposal to Agnes Grey (reflecting possibly the author's own greatest wish of a proposal from William Weightman) now stands guard over her final resting place, with the waves below rushing across the sands of the South Bay.

Visitors still come on a daily basis to pay their respects to the youngest Brontë sibling, often leaving flowers, and sometimes touching tributes including folded up scraps of paper bearing personal messages and thank you notes addressed to Anne. The original headstone, arranged in haste by Ellen, is now largely worn away, but a horizontal slab below, placed there by the Brontë Society in 2011, repeats the words carved upon it: 'Here lie the remains of Anne Brontë, Daughter of the Revd P Brontë, Incumbent of Haworth, Yorkshire, She died Aged 28 May 28th 1849.'

In fact, as we have seen, Anne was twenty-nine when she died, but whilst this error remains for all to see, Charlotte had others corrected. She could not bring herself to re-visit Anne's final resting place at Scarborough until 1852, and on that visit she found a total of five errors on the head-stone. We know that Charlotte had four of them correct-ed, but not what they were, although a nineteenth century newspaper report states that the date of Anne's death had been left blank in order that it could be filled in later.

The failure to correct this particular error and the three years in which she kept steadfastly away from Scarbor-ough shows the trauma that her last surviving sibling's death brought Charlotte, but on 21st June 1849 she man-aged to pay tribute to Anne in what is probably her finest poem, 'On the Death of Anne Brontë':

'There's little joy in life for me,
And little terror in the grave;
I've lived the parting hour to see,
Of one I would have died to save.
Calmly to watch the failing breath,
Wishing each sigh might be the last;
Longing to see the shade of death
O'er those beloved features cast.
The cloud, the stillness that must part
The darling of my life from me;
And then to thank God from my heart,
To thank him well and fervently;
Although I knew that we had lost
The hope and glory of our life;
And now, benighted, tempest-tossed,
Must bear alone the weary strife.'[1]

This was, of course, the terrible end of a nine month period where Charlotte had also lost her only brother Branwell, with whom she had been incredibly close in childhood, and the sister she had looked up to with something akin to hero worship: Emily. After the death of Emily Brontë at the end of 1848, Charlotte wrote to Ellen Nussey, saying, 'She has died in a time of promise – we saw her torn from life in its prime.'[2]

These lines could be said with even more pertinence about Anne Brontë. Emily wrote very little after completing her masterpiece *Wuthering Heights*, in fact her sole creation in this period was a reworking of an earlier poem. Whilst a letter from her publisher Thomas Cautley Newby intimates that there had at least been talk of a second novel[3], it could be that even if Emily had gone on to enjoy a long life she had already lain down her pen forever, intending her one, great, novel to be her definitive statement to the world.

Anne, on the other hand, was continuing to write and it seems almost certain that had she been spared the curse of consumption she would have created further poems and novels. Anne was truly in a time of promise, and in her prime as a writer, as recognised in the early twentieth century by the celebrated Irish novelist George Moore who, along with his praise for *Agnes Grey*, wrote:

'If Anne Brontë had lived ten years longer, she would have taken a place beside Jane Austen, perhaps even a higher place.'[4]

As we saw in the previous chapter, Anne's final letter, to Ellen showed that she was far from afraid of death, and her only regret was that she was going to die having 'lived to such little purpose', without accomplishing the 'humble and limited' schemes that she had had in her head. The question of these humble plans has exercised my mind since I first read Anne's letters. Humility was one of Anne's chief characteristics, so it is unsurprising that she described them that way, even if they would have seemed grand to others, but just what could they have been? The short answer is that Anne's plans must have related to another work of literature. She was self-aware enough to know that this was where her true talents lay, and the phenomenal success, with the reading public more than the critics, of *The Tenant of Wildfell Hall* had given Anne a chance to write about the things that really mattered to her, confident in the knowledge that her voice would be heard.

This plan seems evident if we look once again at her preface to the second edition of her final novel, in which she lays down her own manifesto by stating, 'My object in writing the following pages was not simply to amuse the Reader, neither was it to gratify my own taste, nor yet to ingratiate myself with the Press and the Public: I wished to tell the truth, for truth always conveys its own moral to those who are able to receive it... Let it not be imagined, however, that I consider myself competent to reform the errors and abuses of society, but only that I would fain contribute my humble quota towards so good an aim, and if I can gain the public ear at all, I would rather whisper a few wholesome truths therein than much soft nonsense.'[5]

There seems no doubt that from that moment on Anne began to plan her next book, and that she would use it to discuss a subject that was very close to her heart, however controversial it may be. It is commonly believed that Anne's last work of creative writing was the long poem she began in dejection on 7th January 1849 and completed in a mood of stoic acceptance on 28th January, the 'Last Lines' that we saw earlier. One question remained however: what if these were not Anne Brontë's last lines at all? I don't believe they were.

As proven by Anne's letter to Ellen Nussey dated 5th April 1849, her ability to write beautiful and expertly-crafted prose was undiminished, and from this letter and the poem referenced above we can see that Anne was all too aware of time's winged chariot drawing near. In these circumstances, the always hard-working Anne would have continued to write for as long as she was physically able, especially as it was an activity which had been second nature to her since her earliest days, as revealed in Charlotte's 'biographical notice' of her sisters:

'The highest stimulus, as well as the liveliest pleasure we had known from childhood upwards, lay in attempts at literary composition.'[6]

It is an undisputed fact that the extant writing we have for Anne Brontë is only a fraction of what she actually wrote. We know, for example, that in their youth she and Emily created a huge prose output relating to their created world of Gondal. In her diary paper of 1841, Anne stated that, 'I am now engaged writing the 4th volume of Sofala Vernon's life.'[7] Sofala, from all we know, was a relatively minor character in the Gondal sagas, and as Anne had written four volumes on her life story, we can calculate how fulsome her writing on this world as a whole must have been. Unfortunately, whilst we have some of their Gondalian poetry (particularly in Emily's case) not a scrap of their prodigious prose juvenilia is now known to survive.

Similarly, Charlotte reported that by July 1848 Anne continued to hear from her old pupils, the Robinsons, almost every day. Quite clearly Anne was writing back to these former charges, Bessy and Mary Robinson, on an almost daily basis too. If we had even some of this sizeable correspondence it would provide an invaluable insight into Anne's time at Thorpe Green Hall, including the reasons for her resignation and the termination of Branwell's employment there, but, alas, not one single letter's whereabouts is known.

I have often asked myself what became of the lost writing of Anne Brontë, whether it be poems, prose or letters. Some, of course, will have crumbled into nothingness in the two centuries since Anne's birth; some will doubtless have been destroyed after Anne's death, which was not an uncommon practice in the Victorian era (Arthur Bell Nicholls asked Ellen Nussey to burn his wife Charlotte's letters, for example, but thankfully for posterity she failed to comply with his demand.) It is also known that some Brontë artefacts, letters and writing were sold around the world during the latter decades of the nineteenth century, whether from private collector to private collector, or via keenly anticipated auctions.

It is also undoubtedly true that there remain Brontë writings in private collections that the wider world knows nothing of, but I and many others have long clung to the hope that even now some of these works will emerge once more into the light. Legacies may be left to the Brontë Parsonage Museum, the true identity of heirlooms may be discovered, and Brontë treasures may even be discovered under floorboards or hidden away, Bertha Rochester-like, in an attic.

Sometimes they may be hiding in plain view within archives, and when it comes to Brontë archives few places, outside of the Brontë Parsonage Museum itself, can be more rewarding than the Brotherton Archives of Leeds University's library. Sir Edward Brotherton, later Lord Brotherton, was a philanthropist who helped a number of enterprises throughout Yorkshire in the first part of the twentieth century. Sir Edward's story is a remarkable one itself; coming from very humble origins he educated himself, and by the age of twenty-two he had progressed from working in a chemicals factory to owning it. He soon became a leading industrialist, but one noted for his beneficence to his workers, in sharp contrast to some of the mill owners known to the Brontës during their time.

He was also a keen patron of literature and the arts, and his greatest legacy was the gift of one hundred thousand pounds (then a huge sum) made to Leeds University in 1927 for the creation of a Brotherton Library. It is a beautiful building, and it also houses the late Lord Brotherton's private collection of books and manuscripts, including an incredibly rare and valuable first folio of Shakespeare's plays. He was also, as befits a man who had made his home and fortune in the West Riding of Yorkshire, despite being Lancashire born, a Brontë enthusiast, which is why the library's special collection now houses a magnificent collection of Brontë writings, including letters, sketches and poems by Branwell Brontë and the highly illuminating correspondence of Ellen Nussey.

In 2017, I visited the library to examine a volume which had a very intriguing catalogue record. It contained a number of poems by Charlotte Brontë which had been copied out in hand by her widower, Arthur Bell Nicholls, but it was also recorded as containing an essay by an unknown author, possibly a Brontë.

After seating myself in the Special Collections Research Centre and being brought the requested manuscript, itself contained within a cardboard folder, I withdrew the notebook and opened its cover carefully. As promised, I was greeted by the sight of Charlotte's verse in her husband's hand, which was then followed by a succession of blank pages. Interesting as these were, I turned the notebook over, transforming the back into the front, opened the cover again, and was hit by an electric charge of excitement, as if I had suddenly been plugged into the middle of the nineteenth century.

Turning the pages eagerly, I discovered ten of them filled with fine black ink which had faded with age to an almost pencil-like appearance. The opening line was unfamiliar to me, 'What! Have I actually caught you poring over your Bible,' and as I calmed my excitement and read on, I knew I had found what I had long suspected was out there: a work by Anne Brontë that had never been published in a book, that had remained hidden and virtually unheralded since it came into the collection upon the passing of Lord Brotherton.

I had encountered Anne Brontë's handwriting previously on a number of occasions, at the Brontë Parsonage Museum Library and at the British Library in London. Once seen it is easily remembered; she was a fastidious and neat writer, particularly when compared to her sister Emily, with regular spacing between words and lines, and the use of long straight writing throughout. The subject matter of the piece was also fully in keeping with Anne's temperament and character, providing as it did a frank discussion on religious and philosophical matters.

The form of the manuscript, however, was completely different to anything else that I had seen from the pens of the Brontës, as it was not in the form of poetry or prose, but rather a dialogue between two characters – a dramatic discourse of sorts. There was little doubt that this was an unknown work by Anne Brontë, but I needed expert corroboration, so I contacted Jean Elliott of Elliott Analysis, one of Yorkshire's leading handwriting analysts with a wealth of experience in her field.

Without revealing the specific purpose of my enquiry, or the identities of any of the authors, I sent Jean three images from pages within the Brotherton Library document, and three samples of writing which, unbeknownst to her, were verified examples of the writing of Charlotte, Emily and Anne Brontë. After studying the samples, Jean confirmed that without doubt the samples from the Leeds archives were by the same hand as my sample B – an extract from a letter written by Anne Brontë to Ellen Nussey.

What we undoubtedly have then is a ten page essay by Anne Brontë, unfinished for reasons that we will look at later, and unlike anything else she wrote, but still fascinating and revealing. I believe that this is the last piece of prose that Anne produced in her life, perhaps the last writing of any kind that she committed to paper, and this gives it immense value when we think of Anne's life, and what might have been if she had not been taken away with such untimely haste.

In this essay, we see Anne dealing with matters of religion, and with her typical insistence on the honest truth she also looks at evolutionary theories that were hugely controversial at this time; this was, after all, still over ten years before Charles Darwin sent a shock wave through the nineteenth century with his book *On the Origin of Species*. We see Anne's great intellectual ability and learning even clearer than we do in her novels, and yet we also get a veiled insight into family life within that famous moorside parsonage.

We will examine shortly what Anne was saying in her essay, the impact its discovery had upon Charlotte Brontë, what it reveals about Anne's future plans, and why I believe that this is Anne's final writing. Before all that, let's take a look at the essay itself, as we read Anne Brontë's discourse between S and C.

The Last Words of Anne Brontë

S: What! Have I actually caught you poring over your Bible: here in your study, surrounded by so many tempting volumes? My dear C – it is most surprising that a man of your information and discernment should not yet have cast aside the prejudices instilled into him by his nurse and mother.

C: And is it because your mother has taught you to believe in the Bible, that you refuse to credit it?

S: Not precisely, but because my mother taught me this doctrine, I was doubly anxious to examine it for myself, when I came to years of discretion, and doubly careful against being crippled by early prejudice. And as I found the holy book was full of inconsistencies, both with itself, and with what is evident to our senses and our reasoning faculties, I was constrained to abandon it, though some of its doctrines, I acknowledge, are good, and some of its passages and sentiments are sublime and beautiful to an amazing degree: insomuch that I have often felt half persuaded that the whole was true and even wished it to be so for your sake.

C: And I (God forgive me!) have sometimes almost wished it was fake for yours.

S: And well you might, for if not, your doctrine dooms me to eternal perdition.

C: God forbid that I should think so! No S – you do not know my doctrine. Intimate as we have been from our childhood, we have always been strangely reserved upon the subject of Religion; though you cannot imagine what secret misery I have felt, at the gradual and incidental discovery of your infidelity. But now, since we have broken the ice, let us go on conversing upon this most interesting topic; not as wrangling opponents but as humble and earnest enquirers after truth. Do you state your objections against revealed Religion; and I will endeavour to answer them.

S: To give all my objections were an endless task; but just turn to the first chapter of Genesis; and lo! What absurdity stares you in the face, at the very commencement of that book which you believe to be the word of God!

C: Well! I see "In the beginning, God created the heaven and the earth." What absurdity is there in that?

S: None certainly. I know that heaven and earth must have had a beginning; and that they have owed their creation to some inconceivably wise and powerful being, whom if you please you may call God: but who is God? and when, and how did he create them?

C: That I cannot tell.

S: What, does not your infallible guide inform you that he did it by his word; and that all was completed in six days?

C: But you cannot suppose that it is intended to be literally understood, that the Deity actually produced those effects, by the use of articulate words?

S: No perhaps not. But the time? How answer you that? You, who but the other day were conversing with me so rationally upon the subject of fossil remains, how can you reconcile the formation of the primary, secondary and tertiary strata with the alleged fact of the world's having been created in six days?

C: You think you have passed me already, but I flatter myself I shall be able to get over this, and everything else you can advance against me, to my own satisfaction at least, and if not to yours let the failure be imputed to my defective powers of argument, or my inability to express my thoughts, and not to the untenable nature of the doctrines I defend. I believe I have pondered on these subjects as much as yourself, and I scarcely think there is any objection you could raise, which has not already occurred to me, and been refuted in my own mind.

S: But tell me, did you not always wish your favourite opinions to be true; and always endeavour to persuade yourself they were so?

C: I always wished them to be true indeed; but for all that, I do not think I found it any easier to persuade myself that they were so; for I am not one of those sanguine persons whose belief is guided by their wishes; on the contrary, the very fact of wishing a thing to be true, always tends to make me doubt it. For instance, I seldom can believe in the affection of my dearest friends, till it is proved beyond a doubt; and when I greatly desire an event to take place, reasons why it should not happen crowd into my mind, that on a matter in which my feelings were less interested, would never occur to me; and that appears to me highly improbable, which to a more indifferent observer, would seem little short of a certainty. But to return to your objection – let me first remind you, that the expression a day is frequently used in the Bible to denote a thousand years; or an indefinite period such as "the day of adversity", "the day of prosperity", "if thou hadst known at least in this thy day." Now why should it not here signify, "and the evening, and the morning" (as the commencement and the close of this state of things) were the first thousand years; as the first period? Let us take Sir Humphry Davy's theory found in his last days of a philosopher; I know not any more sensible or philosophical view of the geological history of the earliest stages of the world we inhabit, and it contains not one statement that actually contradicts the concise and simple account given by Moses; though as he rightly intimates the scriptures were written not to teach us "systems of philosophy, but the laws of life and morals". "The ideas," says he "transmitted to or presented by Moses respecting the origins of the world and of man, were of the most simple kind; and such as suited the early state of society; but though general and simple truths, yet clothed in a language and suited to the ideas of a rude and uninstructed people." Since I have the book here, I will read you the hypothesis in his own words: first premising that the theory is founded on the supposition that there is a central fire in the globe; which will satisfactorily account not only for volcanic eruptions, and the various revolutions consequent upon them, but for the ascertained fact of the heat's increasing the deeper we penetrate towards the centre, and the various warm sources, arising from great depths in almost every country, and also for the higher temperatures of the earth in its earliest stages, before the creation of man, which seems evident from the nature of the vegetable and animal remains. "Astronomical deductions" says the philosopher, "and actual measures by triangulations prove that the globe is an oblate spheroid flattened at the poles; and this form we know, by strict mathematical demonstrations, is precisely the one which a fluid body revolving round its axis, and become solid at its surface by the slow disruption of its heat or other causes, would assume. I suppose, therefore, that the globe, in the first state in which the imagination can venture to consider it, was a fluid mass with an immense atmosphere revolving in space round the sun, and that by its cooling, a portion of its atmosphere was condensed in water which occupied a part of its surface. In this state, no form of life, such as now belong to our system, could have inhabited it; and I suppose the crystalline rocks which contain no vestiges of a former order of things, were the results of its first consolidation on its surface. Upon the further cooling, the water which more or less had covered it, contracted; depositions took place, shellfish and coral insects of the first creation began their labours; and islands appeared in the midst of the oceans, raised from the deep by the productive energies of millions of zoophites. These islands became covered with vegetables fitted to bear a high temperature, such as palms and various species of plant similar to those which now exist in the hottest parts of the world. And the submarine rocks or shores of these formations of land became covered with aquatic vegetables, on which various species of shellfish and common fishes found their nourishment. The fluids of the globe in cooling deposited a large quantity of the materials they held in solution, and these deposits agglutinating together the sand, the immense masses of coral rocks, and some of the shells and fishes found around the shores of the primitive lands, produced the first order of secondary rocks. As the temperature of the globe became lower, species of the oviperous reptiles were created to inhabit it: and the turtle, crocodile, and various gigantic animals of the same kind seem to have haunted the bays and waters of the primitive lands. But in this state of things of things there was no order of events similar to the present, the crust of the globe was exceedingly slender, and the source of fire a small distance from the surface. In consequence of contraction in one part of the mass, cavities were opened, which caused the entrance of water, and immense volcanic explosions took place, raising one part of the surface, depressing another, producing mountains, and causing new and extensive depositions from the primitive ocean. Changes of this kind must have been extremely frequent in the early epochs of nature; and the only living forms of which the remains are found in the strata that are the monuments of these changes, are those of plants, fishes, birds, and oviperous reptiles, which seem most fitted to exist in such a war of the elements. When these revolutions became less frequent, and the globe became still more cooled, and the inequalities of its temperature preserved by the mountain chains, more perfect animals became its inhabitants, many of which, such as the mammoth, megalonix, megatherium, and gigantic hyena, are now extinct. At this period, the temperature of the ocean seems to have been not much higher than it is at present, and the changes produced by the occasional eruptions of it have left no consolidated rocks. Yet one of these eruptions appears to have been of great extent and some duration, and seems to have been the cause of those immense quantities of water worn stones, gravel, and sand, which are usually called diluvian remains; and it is probable that this effect was connected with the elevation of a new continent in the southern hemisphere by volcanic fire. When the system of things became so permanent that the tremendous revolutions depending upon the destruction of the equilibrium between the heating and cooling agencies were no longer to be dreaded, the creation of man took place."

Now from Genesis we learn that at first "the earth was without form and void, and darkness was upon the face of the deep; and the spirit of God moved upon the face of the waters." The waters I here take to signify the atmosphere or rather the gasses which are the elements of both air and water. This I imagine will explain the sixth and two following verses which I suppose relate to the formation of water properly so called and the atmosphere as it now is; but first we read that light was created as the principal of light and heat which I suppose held the chaotic mass in solution

*** *Here the writing ends* ***

The Message in Anne
Brontë's Last Words

THIS IS A piece of writing by Anne Brontë unlike anything else that she, or her sisters, produced and the first question it raises is: just who exactly are the mysterious S and C who are carrying out this discourse?

Owing to its overtly religious tones, the first thought may be that this represents the age-old confrontation between good and evil, personified in Anne's mind and her essay by Satan and Christ. If this is the case however, we find a rather more benign Satan than the one we usually picture, one who is on friendly terms with Christ. Nevertheless, this could be Anne's retelling of the story of Satan's tempting of Christ in the wilderness, in which he tries to beguile Christ by tricking him into admitting that the words of scripture can no longer be accepted as 'gospel truth'.

For reasons that we will see, however, there also seems to be a clear correlation between the characters S and C and Emily and Anne Brontë respectively, and whilst there were disagreements between them from time to time, as in any sibling relationship, we know that they remained close to each other throughout their lives; Anne would not have associated Emily with Satan, even tenuously, and so we have to find another interpretation of these two characters.

The most fitting explanation seems to be that the two protagonists were involved in a battle that was beginning to take on greater significance in the mid-nineteenth century, and which still rages today – the conflict between Science and the Church. This conflict reached its zenith with the publication of Charles Darwin's evolutionary masterpiece in November 1859, but rapid advances in science and technology throughout the first half of the nineteenth century were already causing many people to re-assess their faith, and the literal truth of the words of the Bible was increasingly being questioned.

Anne Brontë was fiercely intelligent, and spent her whole life on a personal quest to increase her knowledge, particularly when it came to matters of scripture. She was the only Brontë sibling who could read Latin and Greek fluently, and this allowed her to study early forms of the Bible, enabling her to reach conclusions that would have shocked many who held established church beliefs. We see this in *The Tenant of Wildfell Hall*, when Helen is debating the true scriptural meaning of the word 'eternal' with her aunt who had declared that sinners will be thrown into an 'unquenchable fire' for ever:

"'Not for ever,' I exclaimed, "only til he has paid the uttermost farthing…"

"Oh, Helen! Where did you learn all this?"

"In the Bible, aunt. I have searched it through, and found nearly thirty passages, all tending to support the same theory."

"And is that the use you make of your Bible? And did you find no passages tending to prove the danger and the falsity of such a belief?"

"No: I found, indeed, some passages that, taken by themselves, might seem to contradict that opinion; but they will all bear a different construction to that which is commonly given, and in most the only difficulty is in the word which we translate 'everlasting' or 'eternal.' I don't know the Greek, but I believe it strictly means for ages, and might signify either endless or long-enduring.'"[1]

There is then a clear correlation between Helen, the eponymous tenant of Wildfell Hall, and the C of Anne's essay, and they both reflect Anne's deep knowledge of the Bible's true meaning as she saw it, and her willingness to engage anyone in debate upon it.

Like many of her contemporaries, it was clear to Anne that there was no geological evidence that Noah's flood had ever taken place, and she also understood that pale-ontological discoveries were disproving elements of the creation stories given in the book of Genesis. Neverthe-less, the plethora of scientific discoveries at this time strengthened Anne's faith rather than diminished it, and it is this that lies at the heart of her final essay. She is happy to debate any questions that science raised, safe in the knowledge that her deep understanding of scripture and her granite-like faith could withstand any problems that are placed in her path by new discoveries from the scientific world. For Anne, and for her protagonist C, sci-ence and the Church don't have to be mutually exclusive belief systems.

In C we see an autobiographical portrait of the author herself, just as Agnes Grey was in the novel of the same name, and this essay, brief though it is, contains a number of elements relating to family life in Haworth Parsonage. S upbraids C for still standing by the prejudices instilled in them by their 'nurse and mother.' As in *Agnes Grey*, mentions of a mother here are in fact references to Aunt Branwell, who had become a mother figure to the Brontë siblings in general and to Anne in particular.

We know that faith was very important to Anne Branwell, coming as she did from a family who were instrumental in the spread of Methodism in Penzance, and so it seems certain that it was her aunt who instilled the love of Bible study into young Anne. In her essay, S mocks C for continuing this practice, even when there are, to them, much more interesting secular books available to read.

This is one of the clues to the identity of S, showing us that in reality they are representing the views, and perhaps real life conversations, of Emily Brontë.

As a child Emily attended the Church of England services at Haworth's St. Michael's and All Angels Church, as would be expected of course from the minister's daughter, but descriptions of her manner within church in her youth show someone who was less than impressed by the ceremony of organised religion. One parishioner who saw her there, remembered, 'the stolid stoical manner of Emily as she sat bolt upright in the corner of the pew, as motionless as a statue', with a 'compressed mouth and drooping eyelids.'[2]

As Emily grew older she retained her faith, as evidenced in her great poem 'No Coward Soul Am I', but it is a faith of her own design, rather than one strictly adhering to set laws and structures, which is why in adulthood Emily stopped attending church. For her, the deity and faith was to be found in the natural world, a world becoming increasingly examined and understood in the first half of the nineteenth century – the world of science.

Despite these opposed belief systems, Emily and Anne Brontë remained incredibly close from cradle to grave, and we see this referred to near the beginning of the essay, as C reveals:

'No S – you do not know my doctrine. Intimate as we have been from our childhood, we have always been strangely reserved upon the subject of Religion; though you cannot imagine what secret misery I have felt, at the gradual, and incidental discovery of your infidelity.'

This is one of the most revealing sections of the essay, showing for the first time the impact that Emily's estrangement from the official church had on Anne. The secret misery that Anne reveals here is characteristic of her ability to internalise emotions, withholding her true feelings from her siblings if she felt their exposure could hurt them. Anne had earlier expressed this trait of hers at the close of her poem 'Self Congratulation' which we encountered in chapter four:

'And yet my comrades marked it not,
My voice was still the same;
They saw me smile, and o'er my face –
No signs of sadness came;
They little knew my hidden thoughts
And they will never know
The anguish of my drooping heart,
The bitter aching woe!'[3]

We also have evidence of the veracity of this scene played out in Anne's essay, in a description of a visit to the Parsonage by Charlotte's close friend, Mary Taylor. Mary was a very strong-minded and forthright woman, as shown in her portrayal as Rose York in Charlotte's novel *Shirley*. During this visit Charlotte had been questioning Mary about her religious beliefs, to which she responded that 'religious opinions were between the individual and God'; the usually taciturn Emily then added her support, saying 'that's right!'[4]

We can see that although Anne and Emily enjoyed a twin-like closeness, on matters of religion they remained tight-lipped, so why should Anne choose to examine their respective opinions in prose when the likelihood would be that Emily herself would read it and possibly be upset by it? The answer, sadly, is that by the time Anne wrote this dialogue her beloved sister was dead, and this gave Anne the freedom to discuss their relationship in a way that she had never felt able to before.

It is unsurprising that Emily, always reserved by nature, would choose not to talk about her personal faith with her siblings, but it may seem slightly more surprising to see Anne, under the guise of C in her essay, proclaim 'you do not know my doctrine'.

The truth was that Anne too had developed her own faith system which was not in accord with the prevailing Calvinist views of the Church of England at this time. We have seen an earlier example of this when as a schoolgirl she turned to Moravian priest James la Trobe on what could have been her deathbed, and she continued to cherish the Moravian belief in an ultimately forgiving God, rather than one who condemned people to everlasting damnation.

Evidence of this is to be found in a letter that Anne Brontë wrote to Reverend David Thom, in response to his, now lost, letter in praise of *The Tenant of Wildfell Hall*:

'I have seen so little of controversial Theology that I was not aware the doctrine of Universal Salvation had so able and ardent an advocate as yourself; but I have cherished it from my very childhood – with a trembling hope at first, and afterwards with a firm and glad conviction of its truth. I drew it secretly from my own heart and from the word of God before I knew that any other held it. And since then it has ever been a source of true delight to me to find the same views either timidly suggested or boldly advocated by benevolent and thoughtful minds; and I now believe there are many more believers than professors in that consoling creed.'[5]

Note the use of the word 'doctrine' in her letter to Reverend Thom, a word also conspicuous in the discourse between S and C above. The letter was written on 30th December 1848, just 11 days after Emily Brontë's death. Only now can Anne talk of the belief that she has drawn secretly from her own heart, the doctrine that was unknown even to the person closest to her in the world.

By the time of this letter, Anne knew that she was desperately ill, and although she had not yet been formally diagnosed, it was clear to all around her that she too had the disease which had so cruelly consumed Emily, and Branwell before her. Even at this point, however, it remained possible that Anne could live a further few months, maybe even longer, and so her mind began to turn to her legacy – forming the 'humble schemes for future practice' that she referenced in her final letter to Ellen Nussey.

Just what were these plans, 'humble and limited' though Anne described them? Teaching and the life of a governess held no appeal for her, so, as we saw earlier, it can only be a work of fiction that she was planning; one that fulfilled the manifesto that she had laid out in her preface to the second edition of *The Tenant of Wildfell Hall*, to tell the truth at all costs, and to let the truth convey its own moral message to those who could hear it.

As is clear from her letter to Reverend Thom, her own doctrine, her belief in a loving God and the availability of universal salvation, was very much at the front of her mind at this time, and I believe that the essay you have just read is her attempt to explain this creed that she felt was so important, and which could bring comfort to so many people. It is, I believe, the embodiment of her 'humble scheme', a final work in which she will at last explain the beliefs that were at the heart of all she had done.

The format of the essay is unique, in that it is neither poetry nor novel, but is instead a drama-like dialogue. It could be that Anne, if the work had been finished, would have expanded it into a long two person play, or that this is an initial attempt that she would have used as a framework from which to craft a work of prose on the subject.

A further clue to the date of composition of the essay is found in C's lengthy explanation of a book by Humphry Davy, showing how its scientific revelations are still compatible with the content of scripture. The book referred to is Davy's *Last Days of a Philosopher*, and whilst Anne, as C, quotes extensively from it, she also provides her own interpretation of its teachings.

The reference to Davy's book is very telling. Sir Humphry hailed from Penzance in Cornwall, just as Anne's mother Maria had, and he was a contemporary of Anne's uncle Benjamin Branwell who reached the pinnacle of Penzance's social and political strata. It seems likely therefore that the two men knew each other, and that because of this Davy would also have been known to Elizabeth Branwell, Anne's beloved aunt and de facto mother.

Anne would have felt pride that such an illustrious figure at the time had a connection to her mother and aunt's family, or at least their home town, and it may be this that first led her to study Davy's writings. The mention in her essay, however, is not the only time that the great scientist and inventor featured in her work. In *The Tenant of Wildfell Hall*, as we approach the section where Helen's story is finally revealed, Gilbert finds an unfamiliar book in her study:

'There was her desk left open on the little round table beside the high backed chair, with a book laid upon it. Her limited but choice collection of books was almost as familiar to me as my own; but this volume I had not seen before. I took it up. It was Sir Humphry Davy's *Last Days of a Philosopher*.'[6]

Davy's book had clearly grabbed Anne Brontë's attention at the time she was writing her final novel, but at this point it was new to her, whereas at the time of her essay Anne clearly has a deep familiarity with it.

This indicates that the discourse between S and C was composed later than *The Tenant of Wildfell Hall*, placing its creation in the final year of Anne's life, but there is one physical clue in the manuscript itself which allows us to make a more definite assessment. The essay ends abruptly, without even reaching the end of a sentence, although it was obviously intended to be a much longer composition than the two thousand words we are left with. One possibility is that Anne has moved on to another work, or has simply decided not to complete this one, but it seems strange that such a habitually well-organised woman should fail to even complete the paragraph.

The handwriting itself provides a sad clue to the reason for its sudden cessation. The final two words, 'in solution', are much fainter than the preceding script, so it appears likely that this was the point at which Anne was no longer physically able to write.

It is also telling that the unfinished work was kept by Charlotte Brontë after Anne's death, and that it then passed with Charlotte's other belongings to her widower, Arthur Bell Nicholls, after her own untimely passing six years later in 1855. This is how the notebook came to be turned around and then used by Arthur to transcribe some of his beloved Charlotte's verse.

Perhaps it was even this work that Charlotte had in mind when she wrote in September 1850:

'Blameless in deed and almost in thought, there was from her [Anne's] very childhood a tinge of religious melancholy in her mind – this I ever suspected, and I have found, amongst her papers, mournful proofs that such was the case.'[7]

Charlotte had at this time been re-examining the papers of Emily and Anne in preparation for the post-humous re-publication of their work. Coming across the last writing of Anne, and finding that even with her last stroke of the pen she was addressing the nature of faith and religion, it is perhaps understandable that Charlotte should associate it with a religious melancholy, but in fact pondering such matters, and writing about them, was always a joy to Anne.

Anne's essay also gives the lie to Charlotte's protective pronouncement in her 'biographical notice' of Acton Bell that, 'Neither Emily nor Anne was learned; they had no thoughts of filling their pitchers at the well-springs of other minds.'[8]

This is one of the facts that Anne's essay reveals indisputably to us: able to converse with brilliance upon Davy's work, upon the geological origins of the continents, upon Old Testament scripture, and upon extinct mammals such as the megatherium (a kind of prehistoric sloth), Anne was in fact a highly educated woman with a constant thirst for new knowledge.

We can also take from Anne's essay her belief in the ability of science and religion to exist peaceably with each other, despite the growing division at the time between followers of both systems. It is an essay that preaches understanding and tolerance, and in these words, just as she had pledged to do, Anne spoke the truth as she understood it and then left it to others to comprehend its deeper message. These were Anne Brontë's final words – words of hope, words of faith in humanity, words of love, and now, at last, we can all enjoy them.

Brontë Encounters

W E ALL ENCOUNTER the Brontës through their writing, and are enriched for doing so, but many people in the nineteenth century encountered the Brontës face to face. As we have seen, archives can still be richly rewarding when it comes to Brontë investigation, and as well as Anne's essay, their collections of old newspapers and magazines often contain accounts of first person meetings with the Brontë family in their day-to-day lives.

These stories may be relatively mundane or completely magical, but they all serve to give us a greater understanding of what the Brontës were really like. For that reason, before I close this book with a brief epilogue, I have gathered together a collection of these first person accounts so that they can be accessed more easily, and by a wider audience. I have not concerned myself with the accounts of the famous whose views on the Brontë family are already in print, for example the pronouncements of Elizabeth Gaskell, Harriet Martineau and William Makepeace Thackeray. Similarly, this is not the place to look at the pronouncements of Charlotte Brontë's great friends Mary Taylor and Ellen Nussey; the latter could be a book in its own right, and indeed will feature in a forthcoming book by me, *Charlotte & Ellen*.

I wanted to save the records and views of the everyday people who met the Brontës, the memories which are now fading and crumbling in nineteenth century newspapers but which often contain nuggets of gold, and it is these that make up the bulk of this collection of Brontë encounters. The encounters are arranged in order of the date on which they were published, from 1850 right up to, remarkably, 1941 when we hear from probably the last living person who knew the Brontë family of Haworth.

You will find a varied and fascinating collection here, including two interviews with the Brontë's former servant Nancy Garrs. You will also read the surprisingly astute comments from Charlotte Brontë's phrenologist, hear about the kindness shown to a man with no boots, learn about Anne's reputation for handing out buns, Branwell's ability to write with both hands at once and much more, including a first hand account from a surprise guest at Charlotte Brontë's wedding, and an interview with Patrick Brontë himself.

I have strayed from the chronological arrangement in one instance, as I thought it fitting to close this section with a 1910 memory of Anne Brontë that I think perfectly draws our memories of her to a close. Let's step back in time now and hear again the voices of people who were lucky enough to encounter the Brontës:

Matthew Arnold,[1] letter to Frances Lucy Wightman, Fox How, 21st December 1850

At seven came Miss Martineau and Miss Brontë (Jane Eyre); talked to Miss Martineau (who blasphemes frightfully) about the prospects of the Church of England, and, wretched man that I am, promised to go and see her cow-keeping miracles tomorrow – I, who hardly know a cow from a sheep. I talked to Miss Brontë (past thirty and plain, with expressive grey eyes, though) of her curates, of French novels, and her education in a school at Brussels, and sent the lions roaring to their dens at half-past nine, and came to talk to you.

'A Phrenological Study of the Talents and Dispositions of a Lady' [Charlotte Brontë] by Dr. T. P. Brown, 29th June 1851[2]

Temperament for the most part nervous. Brain large, the anterior and superior part remarkably salient. In her domestic relations this lady will be warm and affectionate. In the care of children she will evince judicious kindness, but she is not pleased at seeing them spoiled by over-indulgence. Her fondness for any particular locality would chiefly rest upon the associations connected with it. Her attachments are strong and enduring – indeed, this is a leading element of her character; she is rather circumspect, however, in the choice of her friends, and it is well that she is so, for she will seldom meet with persons whose dispositions approach the standard of excellence with which she can entirely sympathise. Her sense of truth and justice would be offended by any dereliction of duty, and she would in such cases express her disapprobation with warmth and energy; she would not, however, be precipitate in acting thus, and rather than live in a state of hostility with those she could wish to love she would depart from them, although the breaking-off of friendship would be to her a source of great unhappiness.

The careless and unreflecting, whom she would labour to amend, might deem her punctilious and perhaps exacting; not considering that their amendment and not her own gratification prompted her to admonish. She is sensitive and is very anxious to succeed in her undertakings, but is not so sanguine as to the probability of success. She is occasionally inclined to take a gloomier view of things than perhaps the facts of the case justify; she should guard against the effect of this where her affection is engaged, for her sense of her own importance is moderate and not strong enough to steel her heart against disappointment; she has more firmness than self-reliance, and her sense of justice is of a very high order. She is deferential to the aged and those she deems worthy of respect, and possesses much devotional feeling, but dislikes fanaticism and is not given to a belief in supernatural things without questioning the probability of their existence. Money is not her idol : she values it merely for its uses; she would be liberal to the poor and compassionate to the afflicted, and when friendship calls for aid she would struggle even against her own interest to impart the required assistance – indeed, sympathy is a marked characteristic of this organisation.

Is fond of symmetry and proportion, and possesses a good perception of form, and is a good judge of colour. She is endowed with a keen perception of melody and rhythm. Her imitative powers are good, and the faculty which gives manual dexterity is well developed. These powers might have been cultivated with advantage. Is a fair calculator, and her sense of order and arrangement is remarkably good. Whatever this lady has to settle or arrange will be done with precision and taste. She is endowed with an exalted sense of the beautiful and ideal, and longs for perfection. If not a poet her sentiments are poetical, or are at least imbued with that enthusiastic glow which is characteristic of poetical feeling. She is fond of dramatic literature and the drama, especially if it be combined with music.

In its intellectual development this head is very remarkable. The forehead is at once very large and well formed. It bears the stamp of deep thoughtfulness and comprehensive understanding. It is highly philosophical. It exhibits the presence of an intellect at once perspicacious and perspicuous. There is much critical sagacity and fertility in devising resources in situations of difficulty, much originality, with a tendency to speculate and generalise. Possibly this speculative bias may sometimes interfere with the practical efficiency of some of her projects. Yet since she has scarcely an adequate share of self-reliance, and is not sanguine as to the success of her plans, there is reason to suppose that she would attend more closely to particulars, and thereby present the unsatisfactory results of hasty generalisation.

This lady possesses a fine organ of language, and can, if she has done her talents justice by exercise, express her sentiments with clearness, precision, and force – sufficiently eloquent but not verbose. In learning a language she would investigate its spirit and structure. The character of the German language would be well adapted to such an organisation. In analysing the motives of human conduct, this lady would display originality and power; but in her mode of investigating mental science she would naturally be imbued with a metaphysical bias; she would perhaps be sceptical as to the truth of Qale's doctrine. But the study of this doctrine, this new system of mental philosophy, would give additional strength to her excellent understanding by rendering it more practical, more attentive to particulars and contribute to her happiness by imparting to her more correct notions of the dispositions of those whose acquaintance she may wish to cultivate.

Daily News England, 21ˢᵗ August 1857, Patrick Brontë

With regard to the statement that Mr Brontë, in his desire to bring up his children simply and heartily, refused to permit them to eat flesh meat he asserts that Nancy Garrs alleges that the children had meat daily, and as much of the food as they chose. The early article from which they were restrained was butter, but its want was compensated for by what is known in Yorkshire as 'spice-cake,' a description of bread which is the staple food at Christmas for all meals but dinner.

"I did not know that I had an enemy in the world, much less one who would traduce me before my death. Everything in that book [Elizabeth Gaskell's *The Life of Charlotte Brontë*] which relates to my conduct to my family is either false or distorted. I never did commit such acts as are ascribed to me. I stated this in a letter which I sent to Mrs Gaskell, requesting her at the same time to cancel the false statements made about me in her next edition of her book. To this I received no answer than that Mrs Gaskell was unwell, and unable to write."

Bradford Observer, 19th November 1857, 'A Day At Haworth', J. W. F.

It was on a beautiful morning in August that my friend Puzzlecraft and myself set off to visit Haworth… Haworth is five miles from Keighley, the road is up hill most of the way and decidedly uninteresting, as your view is confined to the turnpike, the walls on either side acting as blinders. For two miles, however, before you enter the village you have it in full view, and the thoughts which it suggests are quite sufficient to employ your mind until you reach the bottom of the eminence whereon it stands. Haworth is most peculiarly situated. It is built in a circumspect fashion, up a steep hill, with a brook at the base, the church and parsonage at the top, and beyond that illimitable heather. It is a genuine Yorkshire village, macademized after a fashion, with no particular distinction drawn between the footpath and the road. The houses are of all sizes and shapes, like a wilderness of monkeys; some low-browed and flat-topped, poking themselves prominently forward, like a dowager at a dinner party; others small and spare, crushed out of all form into a corner, like a little man in a crowd or an unprotected female. Queer, quaint and quiet is the old village, reposing lazily against the hill side – yet not unvisited by the progressive principles of the age; for we found two or three shops at the west end garnished with plate-glass windows, and we even discovered the preliminary paraphernalia of a gas company. As we walked slowly up the street, we lighted upon a chemist's shop, with a frame of photographic portraits hung outside. In the centre was the likeness of an elderly gentleman, with white hair, strongly marked but expressive features, and a peculiarly large neckcloth. "Mr Brontë!" we both exclaimed in a breath, although we had neither of us ever seen the gentleman or his portrait. There was such a striking individuality upon the countenance, that we recognised at once the original so plainly painted by Mrs Gaskell. We put up at the 'White Lion' and ordered dinner. Mine host, whose outer man, attired in a cap and a white shooting jacket, was eminently suggestive of terrier-dogs, went off forthwith to the parsonage to summon his maid servant, who had gone to wait upon the rector during the temporary absence of the regular domestic. Presently she came down, and in an unsophisticated Yorkshire fashion, as if anything she had to say was not of the slightest importance, she gave us her few particulars respecting the Brontë family. "Her family had lived at the parsonage for long – she had often been there herself – had seen Mrs Nicholls writing a great deal;

it was when she was writing 'Jane Eyre' – had oft carried large parcels to the post and wondered what was in them – Mrs Nicholls was very small, Miss Emily was bigger a good deal – they were all great walkers, used to go up on to the moor for hours together – had seen Mrs Gaskell but didn't know much about her – Mrs Nicholls had never got the better of a cold she caught going one winter's day onto the moor to the waterfall, cascade Mrs Gaskell called it." We asked her if she thought Mr Brontë would be annoyed if we called upon him: "She didn't know – there had been lots of people there, but he didn't often see any of them." We requested of her to take our cards up to the parsonage, and to say that if Mr Brontë was disengaged there were two gentlemen who would be happy to wait upon him; and, while she delivered the message, we went up to view the house and churchyard, round which cluster now so many mournful and hallowed associations...

Returning to our inn, we received Mr Brontë's invitation to visit him, with which we immediately complied. We were ushered into a small front parlour, and very cordially saluted by the original of the photograph we had seen in the chemist's shop. Truly a most noticeable man is Mr Brontë, and worthy to be the father of such a family. Though now well up in years (he told us his age, but it has escaped our memory), he appears quite hale and fresh, and preaches regularly every Sunday morning. He has a grand face, indicative of a power and energy which are merely mellowed by time, and shaded somewhat mournfully by suffering. One glance at that physiognomy assures you that its possessor has been shaped by nature after a model of his own – a man of strong passions, but stronger self-control; of warm emotions, but adamantine will – a man possibly eccentric, but whose eccentricities merely prove the positive tendency of his being, and the strength and struggles of his soul. This we must say, that we never saw a finer physique, more courteous and gentlemanly bearing, and more sincere and correct feeling than we met in Mr Brontë. Mournful was it to see the venerable man, and to know that of all his children – the gifted, the admired, the affectionate – not one was left. And most mournful was the thought that in this house – in this very room where we now are – those three sisters wrote their books and read their manuscripts to one another; the chair we sat upon they had handled; they have perused those volumes; watched the stars and snow-storms from those windows; their very presence seems still to linger here; and though they rest in yonder gray church, cold and still, we feel their spirits solemnizing and subduing us, and bidding us, beneath the shadow of the dead but deathless daughters, forbear to trench upon the feelings of the father, or to speak, save reverently and low.

After sitting about a quarter of an hour with Mr Brontë, we took a five minutes run on to the moor; then, with one last glance at the vicarage, the church, the graveyard, and the school, we turned homeward. We purchased a couple of photographic portraits of Mr Brontë as we passed the chemist's; and we were just leaving the village when we encountered a comical fellow, with a merry mouth and an eye like a weazel's. He had been a boon companion of poor Branwell, and many strange and characteristic stories did he tell us of their exploits in former days, the which, however, we shall not here record. Let those who have passed away repose in peace: delicacy forbids the blazoning abroad of the failings of the dead, especially when those still live upon whose feelings the repetition of such tales must strangely jar.

To the 'reading public' Jane Eyre, Currer Bell etc, have become as household words; and who does not know, from Mrs Gaskell's painfully interesting biography, of that quiet, quaint, obscure family of genius, who some years ago so suddenly shot up into the literary firmament, but whose light, so rare and brilliant, was no less suddenly quenched in death? Sadder story there is not in English literature than that of the heroic, much-suffering, gifted Yorkshire girl – Charlotte Brontë. To the secluded village of Haworth pilgrims now come from all parts of England, from the continent, and even from beyond the Atlantic: sometimes an American, now a Frenchman or German, not unfrequently a Scotchman, as I learned at the parsonage. Yesterday it was the Duke of Devonshire or Lord Carlisle; to-day an unknown like myself.

Keighley, the station for Haworth, is on the Leeds and Bradford line, about twelve or fourteen miles from the former of these places; Haworth being about three miles from Keighley, uphill nearly all the way, reminding one a little at first of the round by Corstophine-hill, but gradually, as you ascend, assuming a more hilly and wider aspect – moorland extending on every side. Although the road is fringed more or less with houses nearly all the way, there is no stated conveyance, but the pedestrian will not regret this, as the walk will afford him opportunities of noticing the peculiarities of the people among whom Miss Brontë received her first impressions. Like the humbler English everywhere, they are scrupulously clean in all matters pertaining to their households, and, certainly, such washing of floors, scrubbing of doors and door-steps, and cleaning of windows, I never saw as on my way that bright Saturday afternoon from Keighley to Haworth. There can be no doubt that in England, among the class I am speaking of, there is a far higher appreciation of the sanitary virtues of copious applications of water than among a like class in Scotland. Stone being plentiful in the neighbourhood, even mill-stalks are built and country foot paths laid with it, these last everlastingly resonant with the clamping of clogs – which nearly everybody wears. Most of the villagers I spoke to on the way seemed quite familiar with facts relating to the Brontë family, and in a dim half-enlightened way with the mental gifts of Charlotte and the others, as if, to adapt a line in 'In Memoriam',[3] "They darkly thought her great and wise".

Near Haworth I got many little traits of the family, all indicating the kindly and respectful feelings with which its various members are still regarded in the district. One young man belonging to Haworth, whom I overtook, a worker now at one of the Keighley factories, informed me that when a boy he frequently had occasion to be in the parsonage, and was often regaled with a tune on the piano, a pocketful of fruit, etc. Charlotte seemed generally to be considered the most affable, having a smile and a kind word for everybody; Emily and Anne were more reserved, and for that reason not quite so great favourites. Mr Brontë was spoken of by everyone in terms of the highest respect, even by those whom on many occasions he had opposed on ecclesiastical matters, dissent being strong in the vicinity. I had neither the intention nor expectation of seeing him; but the sexton, who acts as guide to the church, etc., having told me that Mr Brontë, when well, was always glad to see strangers, I was vain enough to send up my card, and had the pleasure of a little conversation with the venerable patriarch, now more than eighty years of age, and the sole survivor of his family. He was very kind, and spoke of Scotland, and Burns, more particularly, cordially, and with discrimination. Although frail he enjoys tolerable health, and in general preaches once every Sunday; Mr Nicholls, Charlotte's husband (who is still curate, and whom I saw about the village), doing the principal part of the duty. The parsonage is a plain, two-storied building, with a large grass plot and a few trees in front, divided on two sides from the crowded churchyard by a stone wall. It was with strangely mingled feelings that I stood within those familiar (mentally at least) walls, where Charlotte, the 'oddly-dressed, clever little girl', had, in doubt and secrecy, written 'Jane Eyre' – where Emily, 'mine bonnie love', as her sister delighted to call her, had sat on the parlour rug reading, with the arm round the rough neck of her favourite 'Tartar',[4] and from which all three sisters had so often sallied forth for a lonely walk to the far stretching purple moors above and beyond the parsonage."

Fraser's Magazine, October 1859, 'About The West Riding', Devonia[5]

The attendance was small in the morning, but better in the afternoon, when Mr Brontë preached; owing to his advanced years, he is not able to attend the whole of the service, but comes into church when the afternoon prayers are half over. A most affecting sight, in truth, it is to see him walking down the aisle with feeble steps, and entering his solitary pew, once filled with wife and children, now utterly desolate, while close beside it rises the tombstone inscribed with their names. Full of sorrow and trouble though his life has been, the energy of the last survivor of the race seems not a whit abated; his voice is still loud and clear, his words full of fire, his manner of earnestness. Lucid, nervous, and logical, the style of his preaching belongs to a bye-gone day, when sermons were made more of a study than they are now, and when it was considered quite as necessary to think much and deeply, as to give expression to those thoughts in language not only impressive and eloquent, but vigorous and concise. It would not be easy to give a faithful impression of the impression which Mr Brontë evidently produces upon his hearers, or of his own venerable and striking appearance in the pulpit. He used no notes whatever, and preached for half an hour without ever being at a loss for a word, or betraying the smallest sign of any decay of his intellectual faculties. Very handsome he must have been in his younger days, for traces of beauty most refined and noble in expression, even yet show themselves in his features and in his striking profile. His brow is still unwrinkled; his hair and whiskers snowy white: lines very decided in their character are impressed about the mouth; the eyes are large and penetrating. In manner he is, as may have been gathered from what has been already said, quiet and dignified.

Bradford Observer, 27th June 1861, William Dearden[6]

It is a duty I owe to the memory of my late venerable friend, and in fulfilment of a sacred promise, to place his character in a true light before the world; and this is the more imperatively necessary, because – though Mrs Gaskell has, in her later editions of Charlotte Brontë's life, toned down some of its harsher features in obedience to conviction of their distortion and untruthfulness – it still stands prominently forth in repulsive stoical sternness and misanthropical gloom. My acquaintance with Mr Brontë extends over a long series of years. In the early portion of that acquaintanceship, I had frequent opportunities of seeing him surrounded by his young family at the fireside of his solitary abode, in his wanderings on the hills, and in his visits to Keighley friends. On these occasions, he invariably displayed the greatest kindness and affability, and a most anxious desire to promote the happiness and improvement of his children. This testimony, it is presumed, will have some weight, especially with whose who wish to form a correct estimate of human character.

It will be remembered that Mr Brontë's children were deprived of their mother when they were at a very tender age. We are led to infer from Mrs Gaskell's narrative, that their father – if he felt – at least did not manifest much anxiety about their physical and mental welfare; and we are told that the eldest of the motherless group, then at home, by a sort of premature inspiration, under the feeble wing of a maiden aunt, undertook their almost entire supervision. Branwell – with whom I was on terms of literary intimacy long before his fatal lapse – told me, when accidentally alluding to this painful period of in the history of his family, that his father watched over his little bereaved flock with truly paternal solicitude and affection – that he was their constant guardian and instructor – and that he took a lively interest in all their innocent amusements. Such – before the blight of disgrace fell upon him – is the testimony of Branwell to the domestic conduct of his father. "Alas!" said he to me, many years after that sad event, "had I been what my father earnestly wished and strove to make me, I should not have been the wreck you see me now!" Poor Branwell! May his sad example prove a warning to others to shun the gulf of misery into which he was prematurely plunged! If Mr Brontë had been the cold indifferent stoic he has been represented, the perpetual outflow of love and tenderness in regard to him from the hearts of his children, could not have been naturally expected. An unfeeling father ought not to complain, if he reaps but a scanty harvest of filial duty and affection in return for what he has sown. Love begets love – a saying not the less true, because it is trite.

As Mr Brontë's children grew up, he afforded them every opportunity his limited means would allow of gratifying their tastes either in literature or the fine arts; and many times do I remember meeting him, little Charlotte, and Branwell, in the studio of the late John Bradley, at Keighley, where they hung with close-gazing inspection and silent admiration over some fresh production of the artist's genius. Branwell was a pupil of Bradley's, and, though some of his drawings were creditable and displayed good taste, he would never, I think, on account of his defective vision, have become a first-rate artist. In some departments of literature, and especially in poetry of a highly imaginative kind, he would have excelled…

The cold stoicism attributed to Mr Brontë was apparent only to those who knew him least; beneath this "seeming cloud" beat a heart of the deepest emotions, the effects of whose outflowings, like the waters of a placid hidden brook, were more perceptible in the verdure that marked their course than in the voice they uttered. God, and the objects to whom that good heart swelled forth in loving kindness – and the latter only, perhaps, very imperfectly – know the depth and intensity of its emotions. He was not a prater of good words, but a doer of them, for God's inspection, not man's approbation. Every honest appeal to his sympathy met a ready response. The needy never went empty away from his presence, nor the broken in spirit without consolation.

Chamber's Journal, 22ⁿᵈ February 1868, 'A Winter-Day in Haworth'

Standing beside Charlotte's last resting place, I questioned my conductor respecting her, and found him at once ready and willing to oblige me with all the information in his possession. He had been "but a little boy," he said, when all the family were living, but he remembered the three sisters well, and had often run errands for Mr Patrick. They used to take a great deal of notice of him when he was little; but Miss Annie was his favourite, perhaps because she always paid him so much attention. Baking-day never came round at the parsonage without her remembering to make a little cake or dumpling for him, and she seldom met him without having something good and sweet to bestow on him. Yes, they were a very reserved family, and very peculiar in their habits. The villagers did not see much of them, except on Sundays; and of course nobody knew that the young ladies were writing books, or that they had become famous, until, long after, strange people had begun to come from a distance to see them. And then the letters! What a heap of letters were always brought to the parsonage in those days by the postman! Miss Emily, who is buried here, beside Charlotte, was the strangest of all the family; nobody thought so much of Miss Charlotte herself. Emily never came down into the village, or at least very rarely; but here, through the window, I might see the path by which she used always to go from the parsonage from to the moors. Hundreds of times, when he was a boy, he had watched her go through the stile yonder, followed by her dogs. No matter what the weather was, she loved the moors so much that she must go out upon them, and enjoy the fresh breezes.

When she went away from Haworth, to become a governess, she was taken very ill, and sickened until she was brought home again, and then she very soon recovered. She loved the moors so much, that it would have been a sad thing if she had been buried away from them. Of course I had read Mrs Gaskell's book, and the way in which she had refused to see a doctor until an hour or two before she died.

About Miss Charlotte, he could not tell so much, she was so very reserved; but he remembered seeing her stand, just where he was standing now, that morning when she was married. To his mind, Mr Branwell was the cleverest of the family. A wonderful talker he was, and able to do things which nobody he had ever seen could do. He had seen Branwell sitting in the vestry, talking to his (the sexton's) father, and writing two different letters at the same time. He could take a pen in each hand, and write a letter with each at once. He had seen him do that many times, and had afterwards read the letters written in that way. Yes; it was true that he had come to a sad end, but Mrs Gaskell had not stated the case about him correctly. Haworth people did not like Mrs Gaskell at all. There was a deal of feeling against her for what she had said about Mr Branwell, and the villagers encouraging him to drink. Mrs Gaskell said that he had learned to drink as a boy, and had gone on strengthening his habit; but that was not true. When he was nineteen years old he was secretary to the temperance society in the village, and it was not until after that that he learned to drink. It was not correct that the landlord of the Bull had anything to do with teaching him, though it was quite true that he used to sit in the back parlour there and drink almost constantly of an evening when he was older. But if he could not have got drink there, he would have been sure to have got it somewhere else. But, oh, he was a fine talker Branwell; and such a talker! Ay, and when he was at the worst, he never missed coming to the Sunday school with his sisters. They all used to come regularly. He remembered Mr Branwell's funeral, and Miss Emily's funeral, and of course he remembered Miss Charlotte's and Mr Brontë's. A strange old gentleman was Mr Brontë – Mr Nicholls, who married Miss Charlotte, was very well liked by the people. A true gentleman he was, though very shy and reserved; but how could he help being that, when he had lived so long with such a family? When Mr Brontë died he "put in" for the place; but when he found out there was likely to be opposition, he withdrew, and now he was living in Ireland again, where he had married a second wife. With such pleasant garrulousness did my companion entertain me, even while I stood beside the grave in which 'life's fitful fever' o'er, the bones of Charlotte Brontë rest.

Macmillan's Magazine, **Volume XXII, 1870, Richard Hengist Horne**[7]

A fragile form is now before my minds eye as distinctly as it was in reality more than twenty years ago! The slender figure is seated by a fire in the drawing-room of Mr G. S., the publisher of a novel which had brought the authoress at one bound to the top of popular admiration. There has been a dinner-party, and all the literary men whom the lady had expressed a wish to meet, had been requested to respect the Publisher's desire, and the lady's desire that she should remain 'unknown' as to her public position. Nobody was to know that this was the authoress of 'Jane Eyre'. She was simply Miss Brontë on a visit to the family of her host. The dinner-party went off as gaily as could be expected where several people are afraid of each other without knowing why, and Miss Brontë sat very modestly and rather on her guard, but quietly taking measure of *les monstres de talent*, who were talking and taking wine, and sometimes bantering each other. Once only she issued from her shell, with brightening looks, when somebody made a slightly disparaging remark concerning the Duke of Wellington, for whom Miss Brontë declared she had the highest admiration; and she appeared quite ready to do battle with one gentleman who smilingly suggested that perhaps it was "because the Duke was an Irishman."[8]

Now it should be premised that the writer of these papers had sent a presentation copy of a certain poem, addressed in complimentary, but very earnest terms, to 'the Author of Jane Eyre,' – the lady whose *nom de plume* was 'Currer Bell' and whose real name we are not to know. To this she had replied in a note, which concluded with these words:

"How far the applause of critics has rewarded the author of 'Orion' I do not know; but I think the pleasure he enjoyed in its composition must have been a bounteous meed in itself. You could not, I imagine, have written that poem without at times deriving deep happiness from your work. With sincere thanks for the pleasure it has afforded me, I remain, dear Sir, Yours faithfully, C. Bell."

On joining the ladies in the drawing-room, our host

requested the writer to take a seat beside Miss Brontë. The moment he did so, she turned towards him with the most charming artlessness, exclaiming, "I was so much obliged to you, Mr Horne, for sending me your —" She checked herself with an inward start, having thus at once exploded her Currer Bell secret, by identifying herself with the author of *Jane Eyre*. She looked embarrassed. "Ah, Miss Brontë," whispered the innocent cause of the not very serious misfortune, "you would never do for treasons and stratagems." She nodded acquiescently, but with a degree of vexation and self-reproach. Shortly after this, Mr S, overhearing some conversation between us, which showed that the secret was 'out', took an early opportunity of calling me aside, when he extended both hands with an *et tu Brute* look, and began to complain of my breach of the general understanding. I of course explained what the lady had said, at the naivete of which he was not a little astonished and amused.

A very gentle, brave, and noble spirited woman was Charlotte Brontë. Fragile of form, and tremulous as an aspen leaf, she had an energy of mind, and a heroism of character capable of real things in private life, as admirable as any of the fine delineations in her works of fiction. Nothing she has ever done seems to be more truthful, more magnanimous, and more touching than the brief preface she wrote to a new edition of her sister's novel of 'Withering Heights' [sic].

Leeds Mercury, 25ᵗʰ March 1893,[9] 'Brontë Reminiscences', Nancy Malone (née de Garrs)[10]

Some sixteen or seventeen years ago I went, in the company of a friend, to see an old servant of the Brontës named Malone, who at that time resided at White Abbey, Bradford. In Mrs Gaskell's book she is referred to by her Christian name, Nancy. Her sister Sarah, who afterwards emigrated to America, lived in Mr Brontë's service at the same time. Nancy received us with much cordiality, and spoke of the 'grey old parsonage' at Haworth, and its once famous inmates, with evident pleasure.

Our conversation proceeded very steadily along until I referred to some statement made by Mrs Gaskell, when, instantly, Mrs Malone bounded from her chair, and began to denounce that writer in unsparing tones, declaring that almost every statement made in the Brontë biography to the disparagement of her old master was either altogether false or had only the flimsiest basis of fact to rest upon. She declared that after reading the opening chapters of the book she became so indignant that she could not rest until she had been over to Haworth to ask Mr Brontë to contradict the more scandalous misrepresentations: but the old man, although much perturbed, refused to trouble himself about the matter. Those who have read Mrs Gaskell's book will remember the extraordinary stories she tells of Mr Brontë's inflammable temper: of his tearing into shreds a silk dress belonging to his wife which he did not approve of her wearing; and his sawing off chair backs and firing pistols in the back-yard in his tremendous fits of passion. They will remember, also, the more than Spartan rigour with which he is said to have ruled his household, and his cold and unsympathetic manner towards his gifted children. It is rather singular that Nancy denied nearly all these and other sensational stories told by the gifted biographer. She maintained that Mr Brontë had a calm and even temper, and although somewhat of a recluse, doubtless, still maintained an active interest in the concerns of every member of his family.

The story of the cutting up of the silk dress Mrs Malone especially denounced. Her account of the matter was follows: – Mrs Brontë had bought a buff print dress, which was made up by her dressmaker in the then fashionable style, with balloon sleeves and long waist. When Mr Brontë came to dinner and saw this new dress, he began to banter his wife good-humouredly about it, commenting with special wonder on the marvellous expanse of sleeve. Mrs Brontë took all his raillery in good port, and the meal passed off pleasantly enough. In the afternoon the dress was changed, and left in the bedroom. On going into the apartment some time afterwards, Mrs Brontë found that the beautiful balloon sleeves had disappeared. Remembering the badinage that had passed a few hours before, she was quite aware who had done the ruthless deed, but she did not bewail the departed glories of the garment very much, for she soon re-appeared in the kitchen with it, and laughingly holding it out to view, exclaimed, "Look, Nancy, what master has done! Never mind, it will do for you," and she handed the dress to the delighted Abigail. Soon after this incident Mr Brontë entered the kitchen with a new silk dress piece, which he had bought at Keighley, and which he presented to his wife in place of the one whose monstrous development of sleeve had so strongly moved to action his organ of destructiveness.

Mr Reid[11] in his Monograph endeavours, without success, to show that the lives of the inmates of Haworth parsonage were not so joyless as Mrs Gaskell represents them to have been: and Nancy thoroughly endorses Mr Reid's views. Her sketches of life in the parson's household had indeed few of the sombre tints that predominate in Mrs Gaskell's. Nancy did not present Mr Brontë as a half-tamed savage, of whom all around him lived a chronic state of terror, but a genial, kindly gentleman, whom no one could know without deeply respecting. As for the 'romance,' as she called it, of Mr Brontë always carrying loaded pistols in his pocket, even when seated at his own fireside, and his firing at the outhouses in his mad fury, all this Nancy emphatically denied. During the time of the Luddite riots, when many wild and murderous deeds were done in the West Riding. Mr Brontë, who had often spoken against such lawless conduct, did carry pistols for his protection when he crossed from Thornton on dark winter evenings, and on reaching home might occasionally fire off the old charges; or he might during the daytime try his skill as marksman by firing at his own pigeons, but never did Nancy know him to indulge in the insane freaks described by Mrs Gaskell.

The assertion that Mr Brontë would not allow his children butter, and that they had little animal food provided, Nancy also stated to be false. "Why," said she, laughing derisively, "I was the cook, and if at any time they had no butter on their bread it was because there were good currants in it. Meat the children had every day of their lives, cooked on that very meat-jack you see above your heads, gentlemen. That was Mr Brontë's jack, and after his death it was sent to me. Aye," continued she, with a look which showed she was thinking of the chequered past in her youthful home, "Mr Brontë was one the kindest husbands I ever knew, except my own, and an Irishman, you will know Mr Brontë was. When one of the young ladies told him I was going to be married he came into the kitchen and said, in his pleasantest way, 'Why, Nancy, it true you are going to marry a Pat?' 'Yes, sir,' I replied, 'it is, and if he only proves a tenth part as kind a husband as you are, I shall think myself very happy in having made a Pat my choice.' And I have been happy," she added to us. "My husband is just one of the best men that ever lived; we never have had a word!" "Not one, Nancy?" I exclaimed. "No, not one," she answered, in her positive way. "Then you think Mr Brontë was not hot-tempered as represented by Mrs Gaskell," we said. "Passionate!" exclaimed Nancy; "why he was just the opposite."

"I well remember one summer morning he came into the kitchen and asked me to clean his boots, as he was going to Thornton. Being bothered about some other matters, I forgot. When Mr Brontë called for his boots they were not touched; but he did not fly into a passion: in fact, he did not say a word, he just put on his hat and walked all the way to Thornton and back in his slippers!" Continuing her pleasant chat, Nancy then brought out her Brontë relics. First she took down from the wall and laid before me a letter, framed and glazed like a picture. It was dated 1857, and at the foot was the signature of Mr Brontë. In Mrs Gaskell's book, Nancy and her sister are spoken of as wasteful. In her next conversation with Mr Brontë, Nancy complained of the charge, whereupon the kindly old gentleman comforted his servant's heart by writing the document which she had suspended against the wall for the confusion of all gainsayers. The letter runs as follows: "Haworth, August, 1857. I leave to state to all whom it may concern that Nancy and Sarah Garrs, during the time they were in service, were kind to my children, honest, and not wasteful, but sufficiently careful in regard to food and all other things entrusted to their care. P. Brontë, A.B., Incumbent of Haworth." Round this certificate of character were suspended photographs of Mr Brontë, Miss Brontë, Haworth Church, etc., and these she also brought for our inspection. The expression of the features in Miss Brontë's portrait, which is taken on glass, are altogether pleasanter than that in Mrs Gaskell's book, which always seems to to have something weird and uncanny about it.

Having restored her pictures to their places of honour on the wall, Nancy next brought out the two volumes of poetry issued by Mr Brontë when minister at Harts-head, and also an old brown pamphlet, which turned out to be the sermon referred to in Mrs Gaskell's book. Be-sides these there was an old book, into which Nancy had pasted all sorts of memoranda, cuttings from newspapers etc., relating to the Brontës, the record ending with an ac-count of Mr Brontë's funeral, at which she had attended as a mourner, and a true one, no doubt, as she seems to have held him in great esteem. Having examined all these, Nancy placed them once more in the drawer, from which she then drew forth a little roll, which she handled tenderly and reverently, so that we almost guessed what it contained. It was a letter from Charlotte Brontë, which Nancy said she had had five pounds offered for, "but," she added, "though I am poor, money will not buy it." It is dated July, 1845, and refers to nothing of any great im-portance, being simply an expression of the kindly senti-ments which the Brontës seem to have cherished towards the humbler of their household. As Charlotte Brontë's nurses and the companions of her childhood, Nancy and Sarah would doubtless be esteemed by her. That this was the case was further evidenced from the little books and other presents she had given to Nancy's children. "Here is a little book," said Nancy, "which Miss Brontë went specially over to Bradford to buy," as she held up one of the precious relics.

But those feelings of regard were shown in a still more striking incident. Sarah Garrs was stricken down with fever, and while she lay in a dangerous state in a house a few above that in which were sitting, Charlotte Brontë came to see her, and in spite of all warnings, fell on the bed on which she lay, and bathed her hot face with her sympathetic tears. As a companion picture to this, we may conjure up the touching scene at Haworth Parsonage, when the fiat went forth that Tabitha[12] was to removed from her home at the parsonage. With great difficulty Miss Branwell had succeeded in persuading Mr Brontë to consent to Tabitha's dismissal by urging economical reasons, but there was sturdy rebellion that day amongst the daughters. Tabby had tended them through all their childhood, and now, when she was old and helpless from a fractured limb, they would tend and care for her. They were sad and silent. Meal after meal went away untasted, until at last the cruel edict was removed, and poor old Tabby was suffered to remain.

South Wales Daily News, 4th February 1878, 'Charlotte Brontë's Nurse', Sarah Newsome[13]

Those who have read Mrs Gaskell's "Life of Charlotte Brontë" will doubtless remember the reference there made to two young sisters who were employed in the Brontë family before and at the time of Mrs Brontë's death. Here in Crawfordsville, Iowa, says the *Burlington Hawkeye*, lives the younger of the two, and one who acted in the capacity of nursemaid to the little Brontës.

One October afternoon, two years ago, we crossed over the streets to the quaint old house with grey walls and dormer windows, tapped lightly on the door, and were ushered into the presence of a bright, energetic little English-woman, whose eyes have not grown dim with age, and whose step still retains much of its youthful elasticity. The neat little sitting-room is a regular storehouse of old-time relics, with its high-backed chairs and settees. The cupboard filled with dainty fragile china, and the odd old pictures on the walls are all highly prized as mementoes of the long ago days spent over the sea.

Mrs Newsome is a fluent talker, and speaks with a slight foreign accent. She loves to talk of the time spent in the old parsonage, and exhibits many treasures that prove conclusively that she is no imposter. The pictured face of the gifted Charlotte, neatly framed in gilt, hangs upon the wall. And here is a lock of glossy brown hair, cut from the head whence emanated so many beautiful thoughts. A homely little pincushion fashioned by the childish fingers of her who afterwards wrote "Jane Eyre," and presented as a token of love to her nurse, who, it is said, always held a warm place in Charlotte's affections. A few words written on a paper that has grown yellow with age, shew us a specimen of her beautiful penmanship, and a Bible, which was often used by the father in the pulpit of Haworth church, is also in her possession.

Mrs Newsome was eighteen when she first became an inmate of the family. Branwell, the youngest child, was then nine months old. Charlotte was five. She remained five years, and learned to love the children who afterwards became famous. She says Mrs Brontë would have been a gay little woman under other circumstances, but she was obliged to exist without beauty and ornamentation, for Mr Brontë would tolerate no bright colouring in his home or family attire. She distinctly remembers the incident of Mr Brontë cutting into shreds a brightly coloured silk dress which his wife had been warned to keep out of sight. What wonder was it that Emily and Anne should have written in a morbid strain when when their lives from the earliest period had known nothing of joy or happiness, or that Branwell should have fallen when free from this unnatural home restraint? Yet this old lady will hear nothing that reflects upon the actions of any member of this peculiar family. It is touching to hear her praise each and all. And in a scrapbook are carefully penned every little item in regard to them or their writings which has ever appeared in any of our papers.

In conclusion, we give a letter written to Mrs Newsome some years ago. It is a curious old manuscript, written on paper heavily bordered with black, in token of mourning: "Haworth, 1858. Dear Mrs Newsome – I have duly received your kind letter, and am glad to hear that you and your family are well. May God bless and prosper you all, both in things spiritual and temporal. Since you were with me, many solemn and important changes have taken place in my domestic concerns. When you first came to us, my dear wife and all my dear children were living. All the seven are now dead, and I, bordering on the age of eighty, am left alone, but it is God's will, and to this it is our duty and wisdom to be resigned. You probably little thought the children you nursed upon your knee would be so much noticed by the world. Emily and Anne wrote and published clever books, and Charlotte's fame and writings are known in all parts of the world where genius and learning are held in due estimation. My dear daughter Charlotte was the last child I had living. She married the Rev. Arthur Bell Nicholls, a very worthy clergyman. Their union was a happy one, but was dissolved in a few months by my daughter's death. Her loving husband and

I are left to mourn her irreplaceable loss... I remain, your sincere friend, P. Brontë."

Dewsbury Reporter, 17th January 1880

We have made many enquiries respecting the connection of the subject of this chapter with Dewsbury, but the information obtained is by no means commensurate with the time and pains taken to obtain it. Our thanks, however, are due to those who have done their best to supply what was required, and especially would we name Mrs B. Hepworth, of West Park Street, and Mr Josh. Newsome, of Carlton Grange. From them, and from others who have stipulated that their names shall not be made known, we learn that Mr Brontë was a man of commanding appearance. He was tall and spare, but his figure was good, and he was remarkable for agility and strength. In temper he was hot and impetuous, especially when he saw wrong done, and it was only by the exercise of a resolute will that he at times prevented an outburst. On one occasion his quick temper displayed itself publicly, yet won for him the admiration of those on whose behalf it was aroused. It was on Whit Tuesday in 1810. The children of the Parish Church Sunday School, according to what was an annual custom, walked in procession to Earlsheaton, there to have what was locally known as 'The Sing;' which, among the Churchpeople at all events, was a great event in the village. As the scholars were marching up, a tall and lusty man seeing them approach, deliberately planted himself in their path, and would not move an inch. Mr Brontë, seeing this, walked quickly up, and without a word, seized the fellow by the collar, and by one effort flung him across the road, and then walked by the side of the procession to the Town's Green as if nothing unusual had happened, leaving the obstructionist agape with surprise. The 'Sing' was a decided success, but many of the teachers and scholars were in fear as to the return journey to Dewsbury, for it was reported to them on the Green that revenge would be taken. The procession re-formed, but many of the teachers and elder scholars seemed afraid for their curate. Mr Brontë led the way, evidently expecting the man would again annoy the children, and prepared to do battle for his charges. The obstructionist was near the spot where he was so discomfited, along with several companions, but made no attempt to interfere with either parson or flock. The encounter, one of our informants states, was the subject of conversation in and about Dewsbury for weeks.

Leeds Times, 28th July 1883, 'Branwell Brontë and his Follies', Francis A. Leyland[14]

I regret that Mr Swinburne has thought it right, in his notice of Miss Robinson's 'Emily Brontë', to intensify in strong terms the charges against Branwell with which Mrs Gaskell in the first instance did not hesitate to disfigure her 'Life of Charlotte Brontë', and which Miss Robinson has thought fit to reproduce in her pleasant and well-timed work. Although the biographers of the Brontë family have done their best to destroy the reputation of Branwell for any mental gifts or manly virtues he might at any time have had, there was a better side of his nature, with which the readers of Brontë literature are unacquainted, but which they may know ere long. There can be no doubt that the irregularities of Branwell's young life clashed with the formal manners of the parsonage. It is not surprising that Miss Brontë, in correspondence with a friend, should inform her of the apprehensions she felt respecting her brother. It is certain that Miss Brontë never intended the private concerns of the parsonage to be made known to others. Mr Brontë expressed to me his sorrow that his son's irregularities were made known to the world. That Branwell was miserable I admit; but I deny that his misery was caused by drink, although he sometimes – and towards the close of his life too often – sought oblivion from his own woes in society and indulgence. Yet he was too worthy a member, on many accounts, of the Brontë family to be excluded from it as entirely worthless, reprobate, and lost. I speak from personal knowledge of him, I possess many of his writings in letters and poems, and I hope at no distant day to demonstrate his power, and to dispose of many of the calumnies with which a hasty and ill-considered judgment has overshadowed his memory.

Pall Mall Gazette, 12th December 1884, 'Reminiscences of Haworth – Charlotte Brontë's Nurse', Nancy Wainwright[15]

A few months ago there was received into the Bradford Workhouse an old woman who, for the sake of the precious memory she cherishes, and the associations of which she is the last remaining link, ought to have been saved from such a fate. Her name is Nancy Wainwright, and her claim to public sympathy rests on the fact that she was the nurse of Charlotte Brontë, her sisters Emily and Anne, and the intractable Branwell. Nancy Wainwright, who is in her eighty-second year, is the only person now living who can recall, from personal contact and observation, the precocious childhood and early intellectual yearnings of that little family group which, first in the obscurity of the parsonage at Thornton, and afterwards at the dreary moorside residence at Haworth, showed evidence of that strong genius which was destined to set its mark upon English literature for all time...

Some wooden seats were placed within reach of the fire-glow, and on these from time to time a female inmate or two would come and sit in wistful aimlessness, wondering, perhaps, why their fellow-pauper, Nancy Wainwright, should be accommodated with an armchair while they sat on uncushioned benches, and why she should have visitors to cheer and comfort her while they had to linger on friendless and alone. The cry of a baby drew my attention to a pale-faced woman who sat on one of the beds. I inquired about her, and was informed that she had been forced there to taste life's bitterness because a worthless husband had deserted her for a worthless woman, leaving her to bring her child into the world within the walls of the poorhouse. The woman had been rendering return for shelter by scrubbing the floors, and now, as she pressed her infant to her breast, I sat and talked with Charlotte Brontë's nurse. I shook the hands which had fondled and caressed the Brontë children in their infancy; I listened to the voice which had in turn soothed, chidden, encouraged, and reproved those "marvellous girls;" I looked on the eyes which had looked into those of the authors of 'Jane Eyre,' 'Wuthering Heights,' and 'The Tenant of Wildfell Hall,' and, without giving way to undue sentimentality, could not help feeling that public ingratitude was to some extent answerable to her being in this condition. We can give of our wealth to the support of the remotest descendants of some of our most famous men and women, but no hand is stretched forth to rescue from the degradation of the workhouse one who was near and dear to, and cared for to the last by, the Brontës, of whose household she for many years formed a part. When we consider how little would have sufficed to have kept this woman of over eighty years of age in private comfort for the short portion of life that may remain to her, a sense of shame almost rises within one.

Nancy Wainwright, however, does not bemoan her lot. The only thing that escapes her in the nature of a complaint is the remark that if any of the Brontës had been alive they would not have seen her taken to the workhouse...

Nancy never tires of talking of the Brontës. The remembrance of them is as sunshine to her declining years. She was twelve years of age when Mr Brontë engaged her as nurse girl, Charlotte being her first charge. She acted in the same capacity to Branwell, Emily, and Anne, all of whom were born at Thornton Parsonage. When the family removed to Haworth she accompanied them, remaining with them many years as cook, her younger sister taking her place in the nursery. She has many stories to relate of the kindly disposition of Charlotte, the wilfulness of Branwell, the hot temper of Emily, and the tenderness of Anne. When "distinguished" visitors came, it was always a matter of difficulty to stop Charlotte from silently-stealing into the drawing room, and when they had gone she would criticise their appearance, manner and speech with such cleverness that her father would often laugh heartily in spite of the utmost efforts to restrain himself. "Branwell was a good lad enough," she says, "until the serpent beguiled him," and she thinks he has been "made out to be a good deal worse than he really was." Nancy could "manage him" better than any one else when his fits of fury were upon him, and Branwell seemed to have a real affection for his old nurse. He often wanted to paint her portrait, but she declined on the score that she did not consider herself good looking enough. Of Emily and her dog 'Keeper,' an animal of the bull and mastiff breed, she can tell one or two stories, but none so good as that which Mrs Gaskell relates of the subjugation of the dog when its mistress punished it for taking its repose on the beds…

Nancy tells a story which shows Charlotte's goodness of heart in a strong light. Nancy had a brother who had literary aspirations. He wrote some poems, and went over to Haworth to to submit them to the author of 'Jane Eyre'. This was in the summer of 1853, when she was at the height of her fame. Immediately she saw the young man she said, "Why, you are Nancy's brother", although she had never seen him before. She read his poems, heard all his plans, and after telling him how she and her sisters had published poems at a loss, did her best to dissuade him from this project. The next day she sent him a letter, again urging him not to publish. A few weeks later, the young man received a letter bearing the crest of the Earl of Carlisle, an earnest patron of literature. The letter contained an enclosure of £5. The connection between the visit of Nancy's brother to Haworth and that letter was not far to seek.

Leeds Mercury, 25th March 1893, 'An Interview with the Author of "Jane Eyre"', Frank Peel

About the month of April, 1851 (I think), I found myself one evening at Keighley, without money or friends. The factory I worked at had broken down, and, like most lads, I wandered purposelessly about to kill time. After wandering about the town till nine o'clock at night, the question where should I sleep forced itself upon my attention. Now, I had had at the Mechanics' Institute of a neighbouring town instruction and practice in reciting pieces, and, spurred by hunger and the night air, I resolved to turn my abilities in that way into account by going into the various public-houses and offering to recite to the companies I found there, and then going round with the hat (cap in this case). The first house I went into I got sixpence for once reciting, with an offer that if I would stand on my head and sing a song they would double it. I pocketed the copper and the insult and decamped. Yet, fearing I had not enough to pay for a bed, I plucked courage and tried in another hotel with more success, for one or two of the company assured me that if I waited upon Mr Sam Wild, whose company was then in the town. I should be able do better than pitching in pubs. I then sought out lodgings in a common lodging-house. Being well-dressed – that is for such lodgings – the inmates treated me very respectfully; and one, a travelling glazier, paid for my supper. In doing this he asked me what I was doing there. I told him, and also the advice I had been given about applying to Wild, and then went to bed.

In the morning I found a sad mishap had befallen me – someone had gone off with my boots. I told the landlady, but she said she could not help me, so in my perplexity consulted the glazier, who, after listening to me went out and bought me a pair of 'pushers' – that is, boot fronts with the leg and back cut off. To interview the theatrical manager with these on was out of the question, and on naming my difficulty to the glazier he said, after a little consideration, that he would put me into the way

200

of getting a pair of boots. He said he was going to 'work' Haworth that day, and if I would carry his glass crate he would see me all right. We trudged up the famous village, and then he pointed out a house where there was a lady – 'Miss Charlotte' he called her – who was 'good for a pair of boots' if I told her all my story. He then left me to 'call' the village. I felt my painful position very keenly. I durst not meet the glazier again without having seen 'Charlotte' and eventually I mustered courage to knock at the door and ask for the lady. By and by a lady came, accompanied by another, younger than herself[16]. With some difficulty I managed to tell my tale as I stood at the door, and was then invited into the kitchen and a pot of coffee and some bread and butter were put before me. By the time I had finished my breakfast the lady had returned to the kitchen and put some old boots before me,[17] bidding me to try to fit a pair on. I did so, and found a pair which fitted pretty well. By this time the younger lady also returned into the kitchen. Both sat down, and Miss Charlotte then said, "I have given you breakfast, found you boots, and I am now going to talk to you a bit." She did talk to me, and in a way that made me wish I had never gone.

She said that in nine cases out of ten people adopted my course of life from sheer idleness or gipsy instinct, and not because they had any special talent for theatricals. Did I think I had any talent? I told her I thought I had. Would I give her a specimen? Here was a dilemma! How could I refuse after the kindness with which I had been treated? In great pain, I said I would try to comply with her request. I gave, first, 'Young Lochinvar,' in my best style, and then her look of motherly severity seemed to relax a little. She then began to ask a number of questions about my family and other matters, which I answered as well as

I could. Amongst other things, I told her I had relations at Cleckheaton. and described it and the neighbourhood to her. The younger lady then asked me if I knew any more recitations, and I replied I could give one or two from Shakespeare. Feeling more at ease, I at once recited one or two selections from 'Hamlet', without any remark being made. Miss Charlotte then asked me if I would give the dialogue between Hamlet and his mother, where the Queen says, "Do not for ever with thy veiled lids seek for thy noble father in the dust; thou know'st 'tis common, all that live must die – passing through nature to eternity." I complied as well I could; gave the whole scene without the ladies displaying any special interest in it, until I came to the line where Hamlet says, "I have that within which passeth show; these, but the trappings and the suits of woe," when they both burst out into good-humoured laugh. I dared not ask the cause of this, but I suppose my looks showed my anxiety, and Charlotte said, "I've seen Hamlet played at Bradford, and they made the same mistake you have made in the word 'suite.' Shakespeare never could have used it in that sense – namely, a dress – but in a wider sense, 'suite,' pronounced 'sweet,' meaning that the King, Queen, and all about them were only acting the part of mourners, making their conduct match or harmonise with their supposed recent bereavement – the death of Hamlet's father." I did not venture on any opinion, but said I believed it was in the book. Miss Charlotte said it was, but only showed the ignorant, shortsightedness of those who tampered with Shakespeare's works.

Other criticisms followed in a similar strain, but I have a very vague recollection of them. After advising me to return to work and leave playing to idlers, they showed me to the door, and bid me good-morning. I should state here, to account for what follows, that the persons in the second public-house in which had I the night before been reciting were members of Mr Wild's company, and that they assured me that I should get an engagement with them: so that when the string of questions which Miss Charlotte put after I preferred my request for the boots began to tighten, I saw I had got the engagement, and only required the boots to enable to enter upon it at once.

On leaving the house I sought my friend the glazier, and found him repairing windows just in the hollow of the village. He advised me to return to Keighley at once, and see the manager. I did so, but he had as many as the business would allow of just then. In another week, however, when they commenced the tour of the fairs, he could give me a situation for building and parade business. Unasked, he kindly gave me half a crown, and said I could go behind at night if I wished. It was now getting in the afternoon, and I sought out the members of the company, and told them the result of my application. I did go behind the scenes at night, and I am now getting at what I wish to tell you. The play was called 'The Lear of Private Life' – that is, a sort of domestic copy of 'King Lear.' I assisted in shifting the scenes, and before the last act began the 'Lear' sent me to the money-taker to get a shilling and fetch him some brandy in a pint-pot, for he was "nearly a croaker." It was a 'grand fashionable night,' and there were about a hundred people in the pit, and in coming from the stage to the side-door I had to pass on one side to it, and there, only just within the garden enclosure, and close to where I had to pass, was Miss Brontë and the other lady I had seen the day before at Haworth parsonage! I now felt so guilty of having told Miss Brontë a falsehood about having got the engagement that I should not have ventured to pass her if the actor's words "nearly a croaker" had not rung in my ears. In the walk for the brandy I had time to collect myself, and I decided to walk past the ladies as if I belonged to the establishment. I did so, and also made a very respectful bow to them, which they gracefully returned. I looked through the peep-hole in the wing and saw them leave soon after. It was some years after this before I learned that the lady who had given me the breakfast, the boots, and the scolding was the authoress of 'Jane Eyre.' I was pleased the rascal stole my boots when I learnt I had had an interview with Charlotte Brontë.

The Shipley Times, 28th October 1893, 'The Late Abraham Holroyd and Charlotte Brontë', Abraham Holroyd[18]

You wish me to jot down a few recollections of the Old Bell Chapel at Thornton, but in doing this I must go back a long way. The Brontës left Thornton when I was just five years old, and of course I knew little of them at the time that I lived there. My father, as well as his father, were both Churchmen, and attended Thornton Bell Chapel, and the former always took care that I went with them. Mr Brontë used to come to preach the Sunday school anniversary sermons there after I became a Sunday scholar, and I knew his figure well, but the real minister was the Rev Mr Bishop, who used to come to Clayton every second Sunday evening, and preach in the old workhouse, in what is now called 'Workhouse Fold'. The house was a fine old Elizabethan house.

What I then learned of Mr Brontë was this – that he had been a curate in Dewsbury Church, and had taken a vacancy up at Hartshead Church, which is in the parish of Dewsbury, and, I suppose, a living in the gift of the vicar, though I am not sure of this. The reason he came to Thornton was this, as I remember to have been told. A clergyman named Atkinson was at Thornton, and he had a sweetheart somewhere in the neighbourhood of Clifton or Hartshead. Now, the Rev John Crosse, vicar of Bradford, was a great lover of the Methodists, and the students at Woodhouse Grove were often his invited guests. One of these visitors was a Mr Branwell, and a sister of his came from Penzance to see him and stayed for some time. She was accompanied by a lady cousin of hers, I suppose for safety, or company, as travelling must have been a serious matter before the Battle of Waterloo was fought. Now the late Rev William Morgan, of Christ Church, Bradford, was curate under the Rev Mr Crosse, and it so fell out that Mr Brontë fell in love, as the saying goes, with Miss Branwell, and Mr Morgan with her fair cousin. As Thornton and Bradford were so much nearer to Woodhouse Grove than Hartshead, Mr Brontë offered an exchange of livings with Mr Atkinson, and thus they all got nearer to the fair objects they were desirous of winning for life. I have every reason to believe they were all satisfied with the choice they had made, and lived happily with them. For my part, I never could see why Mrs Gaskell used the words that she did about Mrs Brontë, and that her marriage with Mr Brontë was like throwing cold water on ice. There is not a tittle of evidence to support such an assertion, and the fact of Mr Brontë sending for his wife's sister to take care of the children, after her death at Haworth, disposes of this statement. Surely there was someone nearer than Penzance who would have done as well, if there had not been something like true love between Mr Brontë and his wife.

As to Miss Charlotte Brontë, I never saw her to speak to but once. It was in the summer of 1853. I had sometime before returned from a sixteen years' absence from home, and, while residing in the souther part of the United States, I met with and read her 'Jane Eyre' and 'Shirley.' So, led by curiosity, I one Sunday went to Haworth, with the desire to see the author of such remarkable works. I was late in arriving at the church, and found a pale young man reading the morning service – I think it was Mr G. de Renzy. Mr Brontë was also in the pulpit, for I knew him at once, having seen him before during my childhood at Thornton Church. The sexton, Mr Brown, had given me a very good place for seeing every one in the lower part of the church, and during the singing of the hymn before the sermon, my eyes wandered off in search of the person I had come to see. Face after face I scanned, until at length, in a large square pew near the communion table and under the organ, I saw 'Jane Eyre,' or, rather, I should say, Charlotte Brontë. I had not a doubt of it, for there was not such another face in the whole church; and I called to mind the following conversation in the novel where 'Jane Eyre' lies in a state of prostration at Mr St. John's:

"She is so ill, St. John."

"Ill or well, she would always be plain. The grace and harmony of beauty are quite wanting in those features."[19]

And yet there was great breadth and volume in her forehead; some resemblance to the portraits of Miss Harriet Martineau, I thought, might also be traced. The cheekbones appeared to me rather prominent, but the entire face gave me the idea that she had much goodness and gentleness of disposition, and possibly great power over those with whom she might come in contact. Her dress was very plain. It was a gown without any flounce, and had plain narrow sleeves. Over her shoulders was thrown a velvet cape – also very plain. Her bonnet was neat in appearance, but not in the fashion. I had scarcely finished these reflections ere Mr Brontë came in from the vestry. He spoke to his hearers of the hollowness of all earthly pleasures, the uncertainty and brevity of human life, and advised everyone to seek religion, and therein, he assured them, they would find "that peace of God which passeth all understanding."

At the close of the service I left the church, scarcely knowing which most to admire, 'the old man eloquent,' or his gifted and industrious daughter. I noticed that she did not leave the church until all the congregation had gone; and I was told that it was her invariable custom to wait to the last. I was determined, if possible, to speak to her, and as I had been told she always came out at the back door of the church, I waited there. Every one had left before she came out, and I then told her the object of my visit. It was to present the author of 'Jane Eyre,' a copy of the Common Prayer Book used in the Episcopal Churches in the United States of America. It was a beautifully bound copy, printed in Philadelphia. I told her that I had read and also sold copies of her books in New Orleans, printed by the Harpers, of New York, costing only about one shilling each (25 cents). She asked me if I had brought copies home with me, but I told her I had not, as the Customs Officers would have taken them from me at Liverpool. She admired the Prayer Book and thanked me for it, and said the Harpers, of New York, had never either written to her or sent her any copies of these books of hers, and of which they had sold tens of thousands. As we walked together up the lane to the door of the parsonage, she plied me hard with questions, to all of which I replied, and she seemed much pleased. She also asked me where I was going to stay until my return home, and I told her at Mr Ben Ratcliff's, when she said she was glad, as they were great friends of hers. We then parted by shaking hands, and I never saw her again.

Leeds Mercury, 15th September 1897, 'An Australian Squatter's Recollections of the Brontës', J. S. Horsfall[20]

You have more than once asked me to give my recollections of the Brontë family for the 'Leeds Mercury,' but as my people left Haworth permanently in 1849, when I was only eleven years old, and as many residents in Haworth can remember more of them than I do, what I write will not be of much value. My most vivid remembrances are of Branwell Brontë, who was a great friend of my father's, and whom I distinctly remember one evening at our house reciting from 'Childe Harold,' Byron's fine address to the ocean. I never forgot it. It made a great impression on my mind, and I can remember him now, a little man (compared with my father, who was tall) with light, reddish hair, and wearing spectacles. I remember he took opium, and not being able to find a piece he had in his pocket, he was in a state of great excitement, fearing that he had inadvertently swallowed it. The three sisters I used frequently to meet, passing our house to and from the moors. One or two of them had dark ringlets, and I well remember their great, reddish-brown mastiff, Keeper, as he was a great terror to me and other small school boys. They had a pet spaniel also, called Flossy, I think, who was very friendly, and I often patted the little fellow. I remember old Mr Brontë and the great pulpit, a regular three-decker, I think it was. The churchyard I used at night to scamper through at a great pace when returning home late. It was supposed that ghosts could be seen there after dark, so you may be sure I did not dare to look either to the right or left, but at the moment I got to the stile at the end of the churchyard I ran up the fields all the way home at my utmost speed, and used to count the trees in the gloaming as I went along to discover how near to home I was getting. I firmly believed in ghosts in those days, having read a book called *The Invisible World*, full of the most sensational stories of the reappearances of people who had been murdered, and I think most people in Haworth in those days believed them to be true.

Bradford Daily Telegraph, 31st March 1900, Mrs Briggs

The latest contribution to information about the Brontë family is to be found in this week's 'Methodist Recorder,' which contains an illustrated article setting forth in the dialect a conversation with a couple of Haworth Methodists, Mr and Mrs Richard Briggs, who were the last pair to be married by the Rev. Patrick Brontë. At that time Mr Brontë was childless, blind, and feeble; and the bride and bridegroom had to wait in the vestry for three hours on a Shrove Tuesday morning before the venerable clergyman, then over eighty years of age, was seen coming along the path from the parsonage, supported on one side by his son-in-law, Mr Nicholls, and on the other by the faithful servant of the family, Martha Brown. Mr Brontë recited the marriage ceremony from memory, and at the close, kneeling with the communion rail, he offered a brief extempore prayer, invoking the Divine blessing on the young couple. When a girl Mrs Briggs was a member of the Bible class conducted by Charlotte Brontë, of whom she said to the interviewer – "Eh, she did mak' t' Bible interestin'. She 'ed a map, and she wor as if she cud see t'Isreealites. She had 'em all befoor 'er like, wi' the'r windin' in and out o' t' Wilderness. Eh, she cud talk easy!"

Bradford Daily Telegraph, 26th November 1900, Sarah Wood and Mr Feather

Another contribution to the ever-increasing 'Bronteania' is made by Miss Evelyn E. Parry in the 'Leisure Hour.' During a recent visit to Haworth Miss Parry came across Mr Feather, who was postmaster there in the days of the Brontës, and through whose hands had passed so often the mysterious letters and parcels addressed to 'Currer Bell.' "Many and many a time," he said, as he showed Miss Parry his little kitchen, "has Mr Brontë sat here, and often have I seen Patrick go staggering past this window on his way from the Black Bull.[21]" "Yes, ma'am," he said, in reply to a question, "it was I who sent off Miss Brontë's manuscripts, and I used often to wonder at the bulky parcels which came to and fro." Miss Parry also visited Mrs Sarah Wood, who keeps a little clothier's shop in the village, and has many souvenirs of the Brontë family. "Do I remember the Brontës?" was her greeting. "I should rather think I did. Miss Charlotte was my Sunday-school teacher. She was nice. But Miss Anne was my favourite: such a gentle creature." "And Miss Emily?" Miss Parry asked. "Oh, you see, ma'am, I don't know much about Miss Emily, she was very shy; but Martha loved her: she said she was so kind." One of the most interesting of Mrs Wood's precious relics is an old watering-can or flagon which had been scribbled all over by the Brontës as children. On its smooth surface was scratched in childish characters Charlotte, Emily, Anne and Patrick. Many Bradfordians will no doubt have seen it.

A Memoir With Some Pages of Biography, 1902, George Smith

Charlotte Brontë stayed with us several times. The utmost was, of course, done to entertain and please her. We arranged for dinner-parties, at which artistic and literary notabilities, whom she wished to meet, were present. We took her to places which we thought would interest her – The Times office, the General Post Office, the Bank of England, Newgate, Bedlam. At Newgate she rapidly fixed her attention on an individual prisoner. This was a poor girl with an interesting face, and an expression of the deepest misery. She had, I believe, killed her illegitimate child. Miss Brontë walked up to her, took her hand, and began to talk to her. She was, of course, quickly interrupted by the prison warder with the formula, 'Visitors are not allowed to speak to the prisoners.' Sir David Brewster took her round the Great Exhibition, and made the visit a very interesting one to her. One thing which impressed her very much was the lighted rooms of the newspaper offices in Fleet Street and the Strand, as we drove home in the middle of the night from some City expedition.

On one occasion I took Miss Brontë to the Ladies Gallery of the House of Commons. The Ladies' Gallery of those days was behind the Strangers' Gallery, and from it one could see the eyes of the ladies above, nothing more. I told Miss Brontë that if she felt tired and wished to go away, she had only to look at me – I should know by the expression of her eyes what she meant – and that I would come round for her. After a time I looked and looked. There were many eyes, they all seemed to be flashing signals to me, but much as I admired Miss Brontë's eyes I could not distinguish them from the others. I looked so earnestly from one pair of eyes to another that I am afraid that more than one lady must have regarded me as a rather impudent fellow. At length I went round and took my lady away. I expressed my hope that I did not keep her long waiting, and said something about the difficulty of getting out after I saw her signal. 'I made no signal,' she said. 'I did not wish to come away. Perhaps there were other signals from the Gallery.'

Miss Brontë and her father had a passionate admiration for the Duke of Wellington, and I took her to the Chapel Royal, St. James's, which he generally attended on Sunday, in order that she might see him. We followed him out of the Chapel, and I indulged Miss Brontë by so arranging our walk that she met him twice on his way to Apsley House. I also took her to a Friends' meeting-house in St. Martin's Court, Leicester Square. I am afraid this form of worship afforded her more amusement than edification.

London Daily News, 22nd January 1904, Sarah Hartley

By far the most interesting figure in Haworth in connection with the Brontës was Mrs John Hartley, née Sarah Stoney. She is a typical Yorkshirewoman, sharp, eager, with an excellent memory. Born in 1823, she became at twelve years old a pupil in Emily Brontë's Sunday school class. She told us that Miss Emily taught Bible lessons, as Mr Brontë was such a conscientious pastor that he catechised all the school children himself. The description she gave us of Emily did not altogether coincide with the picture portrayed in 'Emily Brontë' by A. Mary F. Robinson,[22] but no one could possibly doubt Mrs Hartley's veracity. She was present at Emily Brontë's funeral, when Keeper followed sorrowfully after his mistress's body.

She remembered seeing the Rev. A. B. Nicholls and his wife drive past her house on their wedding tour as they crossed the moors into Lancashire on their way to Ireland, the country to which they both belonged. Before many months had passed Mrs Hartley stood as a mourner beside the bride's coffin – the last of the weird sisters.

Burnley Gazette, 21st October 1905, Percy Howker

Mr Howker resided at Stanbury, near Haworth, in Yorkshire. They were well acquainted with the Brontë family. The older end of the family were christened at Haworth Church by the Rev. P. Brontë. Mrs Howker, who was the daughter of a Stanbury councillor, enjoyed a lifelong friendship with the 'Three Sisters of Haworth.' Charlotte Brontë often came to read to Mrs Howker, during her many sicknesses. The latter often acted as letter-carrier between Charlotte and Mr Nicholls, her future husband. One could imagine that, if Mrs Howker had been disposed to open and read those missives, what a light it might have thrown upon a courtship about which we know so little. Who knows but that such an indiscretion on the part of Mrs Howker would have been forgiven.

Leeds Mercury, 21st October 1905, S. A. Hirst

We might have just been deposited in Haworth, and are actually rubbing shoulders with those whose forebears personally knew and, to a certain extent, mixed with, the gifted Brontë family.

We have just addressed a young man who boasts that his father was the only person to take a photograph of the Reverend Patrick Brontë.

After we have crossed a wooden footbridge and ascended the narrow, tortuous main street – a performance ruinous to glacé kid boots – we address an inquiry to a buxom dame whose proud claim is that her father it was who supplied the Brontës with the notepaper for their literary works[23]. Often had he told her how he had walked to and from Keighley so as not to be out of supply of paper, when the kind-hearted sisters might be wanting some; how Miss Charlotte fairly won his esteem by her solicitude over the welfare of his own little family. It also appears that the brother of this good woman was the last person christened by Mr Brontë, who performed the ceremony on his death-bed, after Mr Nicholls had objected on the ground that the infant might not afterwards like the appellation of Brontë, which had been selected by the admiring parents. This brother is now in America, and proud indeed is he of the name he bears.[24]

Sheffield Daily Telegraph, 7th February 1908, 'Where the Brontës Lived', Charles E. Hall

They were the most reserved people I ever knew, always absorbed in themselves and their own occupations. They never talked to anybody – they rarely talked to each other. Not a soul in the district knew that they were literally, or intellectually inclined. In fact, the only remarkable thing about them, to our eyes, was their reserve. Mr Brontë himself was a stern, severe man – a good type of the Puritan parson; and his daughters, though as the clergymen's children they visited the sick and performed correctly other parochial duties, never entered into the intimacies of the people they visited or invited confidences. They themselves were as close as wax.

The fact is I'm afraid we were a bit too coarse for them. And I think Mr Brontë committed a grave error in bringing so delicate a young family into that cold, wild, inhospitable country, where they would not meet a single friend or companion in their own rank or file. It was like trying to bring up four tender plants in the Polar region.

Mr Nicholls, the curate whom Miss Brontë married, stayed in our house for about eighteen months. We did not like him very much. He was what you might call a non-committal sort of a man. His marriage with Charlotte Brontë came upon everybody with a shock of surprise. They formed a great contrast physically. He was a big, dark, burly Irishman; she a slender twig that you could almost have snapped with one hand. I could never really understand why she married him; for, though she used to come to our house to inquire about him and the other curates, she did it, I feel convinced, from a sense of duty, in order to find out whether they were all that they should be in the parish. She certainly never manifested any particular interest in Mr Nicholls. *That*, anybody would say. And I believe the idea that she was marrying the natural successor to her father at the parsonage had some weight with her. There was no doubt, mind you, that Mr Nicholls was very fond of *her*...

Branwell died in my childhood, but one heard a good many stories about his appearances at the 'Black Bull'. He was a merry, well-read, interesting boy, and it was not surprising that the men who gathered at the 'Black Bull' for liquor and entertainment enjoyed his gay company and made him welcome; nor was it surprising that he went there, considering that there was not a lad in the village, of his own social standing, with whom he could have consorted. It was a pity he was not sent away in early life, then all might have been different.

Shipley Times and Express, 16th October 1908, 'Interesting Brontë Reminiscences', Rev. James Chesterton Bradley[25]

One of the curates whom Charlotte Brontë immortalised in 'Shirley,' the Rev. James Chesterton Bradley is still living at Richmond at the age of ninety. He was the original of the 'Rev. David Sweeting,' and he has just been telling a contributor to 'Great Thoughts' that he remembers all the Brontës well.

"The parish where I went to my first curacy, Oakworth, bordered on the Brontë parish of Haworth," he says, "so I frequently saw all the sisters and their father and brother, and had many talks with them." Mr Bradley used to go to Haworth parsonage "for the change and company," and there he met the other curates which Charlotte Brontë has so well described. Concerning the sisters he says: "All the three sisters were very shy, but perhaps Emily and Anne were worse than Charlotte in that respect. The latter, as I remember her, was a lively talker when once drawn out, a girl of about ordinary stature, or perhaps below it, with features neither very dark nor fair, but with striking expressive eyes and mouth. She had a particular way of suddenly lifting her eyes and looking straight at you with a quick, searching glance whilst you spoke to her." Charlotte Brontë always struck Mr Bradley as a "young lady with deep prejudices and of a strong will." Mr Bradley describes the Rev. Patrick Brontë as "not at all a bad sort in most things. But for temper! I really think he had the vilest temper I've ever seen in a man."

He repeated the pistol story, and adds: "I have known him so wild with anger at the merest thing that ran counter to his wish that he would take up the rug from before the fire and and throw it on the flames!" The son he describes as "dreadful" – "a good-hearted fellow when sober and right but too often drinking and wrong to be of any use to those girls in that lonely parsonage."

Yorkshire Evening Post, 13ᵗʰ August 1913, 'Courtship of Charlotte Brontë', John Robinson

The appearance in 'The Times' of the Brontë letters having again directed public attention to the famous authoress of 'Jane Eyre,' a peep at the early days of Charlotte Brontë and a few reminiscences of the old Haworth days are not ill-timed.

It will be news to many that there still lives in Yorkshire one who was present when Charlotte Brontë was married, in 1854, and one who knew her very well. This gentleman is Mr John Robinson, of Wombwell, who, despite the fact that he has passed the Psalmist's allotted span, is still hale and hearty, and, if hardly as nimble as he used to be, still takes the keenest interest in public affairs.

Mr Robinson will be 76 years of age in September. He was born in Stanbury, in the parish of Haworth. He left there when 18 years of age, for York Training College, for further training as a teacher. Mr Robinson went to Wombwell two years later as head teacher of the National School, being then only just over 20 years of age…

Interviewed yesterday by a representative of the 'Yorkshire Evening Post' at the local flower show, of which he is president, Mr Robinson referred with pride to the excellent training and the good advice he received from the Brontë family and the Rev. Arthur Bell Nicholls. "I practically owe what I am and what I have to the Brontë family and the Rev. Arthur Bell Nicholls," he observed.

"Owing to age and other infirmities, Mr Brontë for a

long time before he died did not take any any very active part in anything outside the service at the church at Haworth. The management of the National School and Sunday school was left to a great extent to Charlotte Brontë and to Mr Nicholls, who was the father's curate, and who afterwards married Charlotte.

Through, probably, special notice from Charlotte Brontë, I became a pupil teacher in the National School at Haworth, Mr Brontë and Mr Nicholls signing my apprenticeship indenture. During that apprenticeship I was often in and out of the parsonage, and also at Mr Nicholls' lodgings near to the home of John Brown, father of Martha Brown, frequently mentioned in connection with the Brontës.

Mr Nicholls kindly gave me lessons at his room every Saturday morning. He was no idle manager of a school, and made a practice of attending at the National School every morning to give religious instruction. Charlotte Brontë also took an interest in the needlework of the school, and was the principal support of the girls' Sunday school, and so much was she beloved by those in her class that many remained in attendance at the Sunday school long after their marriage, even when they had children attending the lower classes at the school.

On Mr Nicholls first proposing to Miss Brontë the offer was not received very favourably either by her or her father, and this was great trouble to him. As he is no longer here, I am justified, perhaps, in saying that I never saw a man feel more than he did. I have gone to his rooms for lessons and felt heartily grieved to see his great suffering from what I can only describe as 'love sickness.' He determined to leave the district, and went for some time to be curate at Kirk Smeaton, but there was an impression on my mind, and also on that of Martha Brown, that when it came to his final leaving, Miss Brontë gave him some hope of better days.

It would not do for me to describe the troubles and anxieties of this poor man, with whom I came into close contact, but I can say this, that no kinder-hearted man or one more anxious to see others improve their position in life, ever lived, and I myself – I might say scores besides – have him to thank for putting us in the way to make a way in life instead of remaining where we had been born, which was undoubtedly at one time one of the poorest places in England.

I often watched Miss Brontë when examining the work of the girls in the needlework classes, and also watched her from the Church tower when she was sitting at her writing-desk in the little room over the top of the front door at the parsonage. It was always necessary for her, on account of her short-sightedness, to have her face within a very few inches of the paper.

I prize very much old Mr Brontë's autographed portrait, which was given by him to me as a parting gift, the evening before I left him at 18 years of age, and I shall ever remember the sound and good advice he then gave me. He pointed out the lonely life one had to lead on the edge of the moors, and also what I might come into contact with in the outside world."

Mr Robinson then recalled the marriage of Charlotte and Mr Nicholls: "They were married," observed Mr Robinson, "during my apprenticeship. It was not known in the neighbourhood that the marriage was coming off, and to my surprise, when going past the end of 'Church Fields' to my lessons one morning, old John Brown, the sexton, was waiting for me, and said: 'We want tha to go to t'top of t' 'ill to watch for three parsons coming from t'other hill, coming from Oxenhope. Charlotte and Mr Nicholls are going to be married, and when tha sees Mr Nicholls, Mr Grant, and Mr Sowden[26] coming at t' far hill, tha must get back to t' Parsonage, so's Charlotte and Ellen Nussey can get their things on to go down to t' church.'

I returned with the message, and then was told to get the parish clerk. I found him just beginning to light his kitchen fire, and I had to rush him off, as I knew they would be at the church doors by the time we should get there. He seemed hard of belief. I said, 'Come on, there's no time to waste.'

On the way he said, 'I must stop to lace my boots.' He did so, and just as the clock was going to strike eight, the three clergymen walked into what they called the front door of the old church and Miss Brontë and Miss Nussey walked together in at the back door.

As far as I remember, the only persons present at the ceremony were those I have named.[27] Directly the ceremony was over, and the interested parties had gone to the parsonage, a carriage and pair drove up from Keighley. There was no station at Haworth then. I remember there was a bay horse and a grey one, and in a few moments Miss Brontë and Mr Nicholls, now married, were away on their honeymoon. A message came to me to go to the parsonage for breakfast, and I went.

A large room which had been used for lumber and firewood at the back of the rectory was cleared out and turned into a nice study for Mr Nicholls, and they then resided at the parsonage. I was taken to lessons on Saturdays just as I always had been before Mr Nicholls left for Kirk Smeaton. Mr Brontë's old snuffbox was given to me as a keepsake, and that I have given to the Brontë museum at Haworth. I also got Branwell Brontë's violin, which I have given to a son-in-law of mine."

Mr Robinson cherishes the recollections of his old Haworth days, and some of his property at Wombwell has been named Stanbury Villas and Haworth Place.

Leeds Mercury, 8ᵗʰ January 1926, 'Brontë Family Memories', Sarah Ann Sunderland and Mary Whitaker

Vivid recollections of the Brontë family are possessed by an old Haworth resident, Mrs Sarah Ann Sunderland, aged eighty-five, who lives with her sister, Mrs Mary Whitaker, aged eighty, in a house high up on the Keighley side of Haworth.

When I saw them to-day they told me of the visits Charlotte Brontë (author of 'Jane Eyre' who died at Haworth in 1855) used to pay to the old Haworth Church School when the two sisters were scholars there.

"Charlotte was best known to us," said Mrs Sunderland, "because she used to come into the knitting and sewing classes and inspect our work, praising or pointing out faults. She was, I remember, very short-sighted, and had to hold the work close to her eyes to see it clearly."

Mrs Sunderland described Charlotte Brontë as being small and slender; and in support of the description, told how the caretaker of the Parish Church found one of her gloves, which was so tiny that he could only get two of his fingers inside it.

Mrs Sunderland referred to the Rev. A. B. Nicholls, who later became the husband of Charlotte, as a tall, dark, well-made man. At that time he was curate at Haworth Church. Branwell Brontë, the brother of Charlotte, Mrs

Sunderland says she only knew by seeing him pass up and down the street. "They were a very reserved family," she added.

Leeds Mercury, 7th August 1928, 'Old John of Haworth', John Tooit

'Old John Tooit,' the 85-year-old Haworth man who (as described in the 'Leeds Mercury' yesterday) met Sir James Roberts, an acquaintance of his boyhood days, at the Brontë gathering on Saturday, is a merry-hearted man.

"Ah'll tell tha summat," he said to a colleague. "Ah nivver spak to my wife 'till t'day I married her!"

"Good heavens! What on earth for?" he was asked.

"Because," replied Old John, "she worn't mi wife 'till ah wed 'er."

John worked as a youth in the village barber's shop, and remembers lathering the chin of the Rev. Patrick Brontë.

"One day when 'e wor in t'shop," he said, "e eard old A-cursin' and swearin' awful. 'A-,' says Mr Brontë, 'ye doant find them words in t'Bible. Do you read your Bible?'

"A- says: 'Aw, aye, but we've a book at hooam we tak more gawm on when we've no brass for t'shop.'

"He meant t' credit book," said Old John with a chuckle.

Leeds Mercury, 14th June 1929, 'A Link With The Brontës', John Rushworth

In the village of Denholme there lives one who is very proud of the fact that at one time he knew the Brontë family. He is 95 year old Mr John Rushworth, who went to the Sunday school at Haworth, where Charlotte was a teacher. He remembers her well, but confesses he did not see much of her because "there was a partition between the boys and girls." He has memories of both Emily and Branwell Brontë.

John, who is a native of Haworth, and lives with a son who is himself old enough to draw the old-age pension, claims his liking for milk to be the foundation of his longevity.

Yorkshire Evening Post, 1ˢᵗ January 1936, 'Death of Sir James Roberts', Sir James Roberts BT[28]

The last public function he attended in Yorkshire was on August 4, 1928, when he visited Haworth to hand over the deeds of the Haworth Parsonage, the home of the Brontës, which he had purchased for £3,000 to give to the Brontë Society. In a notable speech which he made on that occasion, he recalled in touching phrase the well-remembered scenes of his childhood:

"I was born in this parish in the same week in which the unhappy Branwell Brontë died: an event followed at intervals of distressing brevity by the deaths of Emily and Anne. It is to me a somewhat melancholy reflection that I am one of the fast narrowing circle of Haworth veterans who remember the Parsonage family.

I heard Mr Brontë preach, and remember him as a man most tolerant to divergencies of religious conviction. Above all these memorabilia there rises before me the frail and unforgettable figure of Charlotte Brontë, who more than once stopped to speak a kindly word to the little lad who now stands a patriarch before you. These early associations, still very dear to me, were followed in after years by exceeding delight in those creations of imaginative genius which Charlotte and her sisters have left to us. I humbly stand in the ranks of the unnumbered and world-wide multitude who have found not only delight but inspiration from these sisters, who, encumbered with many adversities, rose to such great and shining heights of endeavour and discovered to the world their extraordinary literary powers."

Yorkshire Evening Post, 21st January 1941, Anne Tempest

Miss Anne Tempest, of West Lane, Haworth, the oldest inhabitant of the Brontë country, is 96 years of age to-day. She is in good health. A native of Stanbury, the moorland village near Haworth, she remembers seeing Charlotte Brontë walking on the moors accompanied by a little brown curly-haired dog. She does not remember any other members of the family, except the Rev. Patrick Brontë, whom she often saw when she attended Haworth Church School on Sundays. She remembers Mr Brontë's last sermon, which he preached from the three-decker pulpit in church.

When she was 93 years of age, Miss Tempest took part in a broadcast from the Brontë Museum, the title of the broadcast being 'The Quiet House At Haworth.'

Cornhill Magazine, 29th July 1910, 'Old Haworth Folk Who Knew The Brontës', Tabitha Ratcliffe[29]

She still preserves a few mementoes of the various members of the family: of Miss Branwell a silk shawl, of Mr Brontë a small hammer he used to use, and of Charlotte a delaine skirt and a white sprigged net veil – which latter has served as a christening veil for several of her grandchildren. Perhaps, however, her most interesting relic is a photograph on glass of the three sisters. "I believe Charlotte was the lowest and the broadest, and Emily was the tallest. She'd bigger bones and was stronger looking and more masculine, but very nice in her ways," she comments. "But I used to think Miss Anne looked the nicest and most serious like; she used to teach at Sunday school. I've been taught by her and by Charlotte and all." And it is on Anne that her glance rests as she says, "I think that is a good face." There is no doubt which of the sisters of Haworth was Mrs Ratcliffe's favourite.

Epilogue

ANNE BRONTË'S WAS a good face, as Tabitha Ratcliffe said, and she had a good heart to go with it. She was always concerned about the welfare, physical and spiritual, of those she loved, and she extended this care to her readership too.

Anne summed this up perfectly in her preface to the second edition of *The Tenant of Wildfell Hall*, but it can be found running like a rich vein throughout all her work. She loved to give innocent pleasure, and readers throughout the decades have been able to testify to her success in this endeavour, but her priority was always to convey the truth. Anne held up a mirror to society at the time she lived, revealing its fragile beauty and ugly flaws; it was a world full of inequality, based upon class and gender, but when we read her novels today we may find that, beneath the bonnets and crinoline, it is a world that's not too different to our own.

Anne was always on the side of the downtrodden and those who were denied justice, which is why she is in many ways the most radical, and relevant, of the Brontë sisters. If she had lived longer she would doubtless have created further works of brilliance, and would have continued her unflinching examination of society and human relationships.

'If she had lived longer' – the perennial lament of Brontë enthusiasts the world over. Alas, Anne left us with only two novels and fifty-nine poems, although we now also have Anne's unfinished essay, the discourse between

C and S, to add to her oeuvre. It is enough, however, to ensure that she is counted among the very best writers of the nineteenth century, and as each year passes more and more people discover the genius of her work.

Genius is a mantle that fits Anne's shoulders like the shawls she wore on her walks across the moors. She was a brilliant writer, a loving sister and daughter, a fine artist and pianist, and she was a kind-hearted woman who was determined to leave the world a better place because of the fact she had been in it. And she succeeded.

2020 is the perfect year to celebrate Anne Brontë, but her work has a timeless quality. The messages conveyed by the story of Anne's life are timeless too: the importance of love, of fidelity to whatever you believe in, of compassion, above all the importance of the truth and the courage to stand by your truth whatever comes your way.

Anne liked to close her diary papers by looking ahead and imagining what the future would bring. For example, she ended her final diary paper, in 1845, by writing:

'I wonder where we shall all be and where situated on the thirtieth of July 1848 when if we are all alive Emily will be just 30, I shall be in my 29th year, Charlotte in her 33rd and Branwell in his 32nd, and what changes shall we have seen and known and shall we be much changed ourselves? I hope not – for the worse at least… Hoping for the best, I conclude, Anne Brontë'

As I write these final words, fans across the world are preparing to celebrate her 200th birthday, but I wonder what changes will have been seen by the 17th of January 3820 which will mark two thousand years since Anne's birth? The world will be a very different place in ways which we cannot begin to conceive, but if humankind exists it will surely still be reading and loving the novels of Anne Brontë and her sisters. Hoping for the best, I conclude. Thank you for sharing *Crave the Rose,* and this celebration of Anne's life and work, with me.

Notes

Chapter One

1. Brontë, Anne, *Agnes Grey*, p.3.
2. Will of Thomas Branwell, Merchant of Penzance, Cornwall, 1808, National Archives, Kew, London.
3. Letter from Maria Branwell to Patrick Brontë, 18th November 1812, ms. Brontë Parsonage Museum, Haworth.
4. Letter from Patrick Brontë to Elizabeth Gaskell, 16th June 1855, ms. Brontë Parsonage Museum, Haworth.
5. Cornish Telegraph, 25 December 1884.
6. Green, Dudley, *Patrick Brontë Father of Genius*, p. 70.
7. Leeds Intelligencer, 14 June 1819.
8. Archbishop Longley letters archive, Lambeth Palace, London.
9. Letter from Charlotte Brontë to Ellen Nussey, 16th February 1850, ms. Brontë Parsonage Museum, Haworth.
10. Branwell, Maria, *The Advantages of Poverty in Religious Concerns*, ms. Brotherton Library, Leeds.
11. Rhodes, Professor Philip, *A Medical Appraisal of the Brontës*, Brontë Society Transactions, 1972, Volume 16, Issue 2, p. 102.
12. Letter from Patrick Brontë to Elizabeth Gaskell, 20th June 1855.
13. Gaskell, Elizabeth, *The Life of Charlotte Brontë*, p. 95.
14. Brontë, Charlotte, *Jane Eyre*, p. 65.

Chapter Two

1. Patrick was the first Brontë to find his way into print, thanks to two volumes of poetry and an allegorical novel entitled *The Maid of Killarney*.

2. Edgerley, C. Mabel, *Elizabeth Branwell – The "Small, Antiquated Lady"*, Brontë Society Transactions 1937, Volume 9, Issue 2, p. 106.

3. Dinsdale, Ann, *Mrs Brontë's Nurse*, Brontë Studies 2005, Volume 30, Issue 3, p. 258.

4. Gaskell, Elizabeth, *The Life of Charlotte Brontë*, p. 87.

5. Green, Dudley [ed.], *The Letters of the Reverend Patrick Brontë*, p. 43.

6. Nussey, Ellen, *Reminiscences of Charlotte Brontë*, Scribner's Magazine, 1871.

7. Maria Branwell's portrait is one of the Branwell miniatures now housed in the Brontë Parsonage Museum, Haworth.

8. Letter from Ellen Nussey to Elizabeth Gaskell, 15th November 1855, ms. Brotherton Library, Leeds.

9. Leeds Mercury, 11 September 1824.

10. Gaskell, Elizabeth, *The Life of Charlotte Brontë*, p. 147.

11. Letter from Charlotte Brontë to Ellen Nussey, 4th July 1834, ms. Huntingdon Library, San Marino, California.

12. Brontë, Charlotte, *The History of The Year*, 12th March 1829.

13. Gaskell, Elizabeth, *The Life of Charlotte Brontë*, p. 94.

14. Diary paper of Emily and Anne Brontë, 24th November 1834, ms. Brontë Parsonage Museum, Haworth.

15. Brontë, Anne, Verses by Lady Geralda.

16. Ibid.

Chapter Three

1. Edgerley, C. Mabel, *Elizabeth Branwell – The "Small, Antiquated Lady"*, Brontë Society Transactions 1937, Volume 9, Issue 2, p. 107.

2. Letter from Charlotte Brontë to Ellen Nussey, 6th July 1835, ms. Huntingdon Library, San Marino, California.

3. Brontë, Charlotte, *Biographical Notice of Ellis and Acton Bell*, ms. British Library, London.

4. Brontë, Charlotte, *Shirley*, p. 296.

5. Brontë, Charlotte, *Roe Head Journal*, ms. Brontë Parsonage Museum, Haworth.

6. This medal is now in the collection of the Brontë Parsonage Museum, Haworth.

7. Brontë, Anne, Alexander and Zenobia.

8. 'Her restless and romantic mind dwelt with pleasure on the idea of a power to be established in the East, of which she was to be the mistress: – a large fleet was to come from afar to aid this conquest, and her sceptre was to wave with equal glory to that of Zenobia who defended Palmyra'; Carne, John, *Letters From the East*, p. 426.

9. Letter from Ellen Nussey to Elizabeth Gaskell, ms. Brotherton Library, Leeds.

10. Letter from James la Trobe to William Scruton, contained within *Reminiscences of Charlotte Brontë* by Ellen Nussey, Scribner's Magazine, 1871.

11. Patrick Brontë claimed to be too ill to attend the wedding of Charlotte Brontë and Arthur Bell Nicholls on 29th June 1854, so Margaret Wooler took on the role of 'father of the bride'.

12. Brontë, Anne, A Word To The Calvinists.

13. Brontë, Anne, *Agnes Grey*, p. 9.

Chapter Four

1. See the testimony of Tabitha Ratcliffe – the final entry in the Brontë Encounters section of this book.

2. Brontë, Charlotte, *Shirley*, p. 326.

3. Leeds Intelligencer, 11th August 1838.

4. Letter from Charlotte Brontë to Ellen Nussey, 15th April 1839, ms. Huntingdon Library, San Marino, California.

5. From the diary of Gertrude Elizabeth Brooke, published in the Mirfield Parish News.

6. Records show there were 67 deaths in Haworth in 1839 with an average age at death of 25.4; in 1838 it had been just 19.6 years.

7. Brontë, Patrick, *A Funeral Sermon For The Late Rev. William Weightman, M.A.*, ms. Brontë Parsonage Museum, Haworth.

8. Ibid.

9. *The Durham University Calendar For 1842*, p. 63.

10. Letter from Charlotte Brontë to Ellen Nussey, 13th March 1841.

11. Letter from Charlotte Brontë to Ellen Nussey, 20th January 1842.

12. Brontë, Anne, Lines Written At Thorp Green.

13. Letter from Branwell Brontë to Francis Grundy, 25th October 1842.

14. Brontë, Patrick, *A Funeral Sermon For The Late Rev. William Weightman, M.A.*, ms. Brontë Parsonage Museum, Haworth.

Chapter Five

1. Orel, Harold [ed.], *The Brontës: Interviews and Recollections*, p. 25.
2. Letter from Branwell Brontë to Francis Grundy, 29th October 1842.
3. Brontë, Anne, Yes, Thou Art Gone, (the title of this poem was changed to 'A Reminiscence' for its inclusion in *Poems by Currer, Ellis and Acton Bell*).
4. Diary paper of Anne Brontë, 30th July 1841, ms. Law collection.
5. Brontë, Anne, Lines Composed In A Wood On A Windy Day.
6. Diary paper of Anne Brontë, 30th July 1841, ms. Law collection.
7. Brontë, Anne, Home.
8. Grundy, Francis, *Pictures of The Past*, pp. 80-1.
9. Letter from Branwell Brontë to Francis Grundy, October 1845.
10. Diary paper of Anne Brontë, 31st July 1845, ms. Will Self collection.
11. For this account in a letter from Charlotte Brontë to Ellen Nussey, dated 10th December 1848, see chapter six.
12. Diary paper of Emily Brontë, 31st July 1845, ms. Will Self collection.

Chapter Six

1. Diary paper of Anne Brontë, 31st July 1845, ms. Will Self collection.

2. Gérin, Winifred, *Anne Brontë*, p. 238.

3. Grundy, Francis, *Pictures of The Past*, p. 92.

4. Brontë, Charlotte, *Biographical Notice of Ellis and Acton Bell*, ms. British Library, London.

5. Charlotte included this poem in an 1850 anthology of her sisters' verse. She sometimes changed the titles, and on occasion altered or even added a line or two.

6. Brontë, Charlotte, *Biographical Notice of Ellis and Acton Bell*, ms. British Library, London.

7. Letter from Charlotte Brontë to W. S. Williams, 2nd October 1848, ms. Pierpont Morgan Library, New York.

8. Green, Dudley [ed.], *The Letters of The Reverend Patrick Brontë*, p. 44.

9. Brontë, Anne, 'The Arbour', *Poems by Currer, Ellis and Acton Bell*, p. 23.

10. Brontë, Anne, 'Appeal', *Poems by Currer, Ellis and Acton Bell*, p. 121.

11. Brontë, Anne, 'Fluctuations', *Poems by Currer, Ellis and Acton Bell*, p. 142.

12. Brontë, Charlotte, *Biographical Notice of Ellis and Acton Bell*, ms. British Library, London.

13. Hargreaves, G. D., *The Publishing of "Poems by Currer, Ellis and Acton Bell"*, Brontë Society Transactions, 1969, pp. 294-5.

14. Last Will and Testament of Elizabeth Branwell, 30th April 1833, ms. National Archives, London.

15. Letter from Charlotte Brontë to Thomas de Quincey, 16th June 1847, ms. Berg Collection, New York Public Library.

Chapter Seven

1. Brontë, Charlotte, *Biographical Notice of Ellis and Acton Bell*, ms. British Library, London.
2. Diary paper of Anne Brontë, 31st July 1845, ms. Will Self collection.
3. Brontë, Anne, *Agnes Grey*, p. 1.
4. Brontë, Anne, *Agnes Grey*, p. 19.
5. Brontë, Anne, *Agnes Grey*, p. 44.
6. Brontë, Anne, *Agnes Grey*, p. 109.
7. Letter from Charlotte Brontë to Ellen Nussey, 28th July 1848, ms. Brontë Parsonage Museum, Haworth.
8. Letter from Charlotte Brontë to Ellen Nussey, 10th December 1848, ms. Amy Lowell Collection, Harvard University.
9. Brontë, Anne, *Agnes Grey*, p. 76.
10. Letter from Charlotte Brontë to Ellen Nussey, 29th September 1840.
11. Brontë, Anne, *Agnes Grey*, p. 153.
12. Moore, George, *Conversations In Ebury Street*, pp. 219-20.
13. Letter from Charlotte Brontë to Aylott & Jones, 6th April 1846, ms. Brontë Parsonage Museum, Haworth.
14. Anthony Trollope's first novel *The Macdermots of Ballycloran* was published by Newby in 1847, the same year as *Agnes Grey* and *Wuthering Heights*. Like Anne and Emily, Trollope received no payment from the unscrupulous publisher.
15. Evening Mail, 5th December 1859.

Chapter Eight

1. The Atlas, 22nd January 1848, p. 59.
2. Douglas Jerrold's Weekly Newspaper, 15th January 1848, p.77.
3. Brontë, Anne, *The Tenant of Wildfell Hall*, p. 3.
4. Diary paper of Anne Brontë, 31st July 1845, ms. Will Self collection.
5. Langland, Elizabeth, *Anne Brontë: The Other One*, p. 60.
6. Sinclair, May, *Introduction To The Tenant of Wildfell Hall*, p. 1.
7. Brontë, Anne, *The Tenant of Wildfell Hall*, p. 243.
8. Last Will and Testament of Elizabeth Branwell, 30th April 1833, ms. National Archives, London.
9. Letter from Charlotte Brontë to W. S. Williams, 5th September 1850, ms. Parrish Collection, Princeton University.
10. Gérin, Winifred, *Anne Brontë*, p. 261.
11. The Rambler, September 1848.
12. Brontë, Anne, *The Tenant of Wildfell Hall*, p. 3.
13. Smith, George, *A Memoir With Some Pages of Autobiography*, p. 89.
14. Smith, George, *A Memoir With Some Pages of Autobiography*, p. 91.
15. Ibid.
16. Smith, George, *A Memoir With Some Pages of Autobiography*, p. 89.
17. Nussey, Ellen, *Reminiscences of Charlotte Brontë*, Scribner's Magazine, 1871, p. 79.

Chapter Nine

1. Brontë, Anne, *The Tenant of Wildfell Hall*, pp. 4-5.

2. See the account in the diary of John Greenwood, ms. Brontë Parsonage Museum.

3. Du Maurier, Daphne, *The Infernal World of Branwell Brontë*, p. 4.

4. Grundy, Francis, *Pictures of The Past*, p. 92.

5. Brontë, Emily, 'The Old Stoic', *Poems by Currer, Ellis and Acton Bell*, p. 141.

6. Letter from Charlotte Brontë to W.S. Williams, 22nd November 1848, ms. British Library, London.

7. Letter from Charlotte Brontë to Ellen Nussey, 23rd November 1848, ms. Brontë Parsonage Museum.

8. Barker, Juliet, *The Brontës*, p. 580.

9. Letter from Charlotte Brontë to Ellen Nussey, 23rd December 1848, ms. Berg Collection, New York Public Library.

10. Nussey, Ellen, *Reminiscences of Charlotte Brontë*, Scribner's Magazine, 1871.

11. Rhodes, Professor Philip, *A Medical Appraisal of The Brontës*, Brontë Society Transactions, 1972, Volume 16, Issue 2, p. 102.

12. Brontë, Anne, Last Lines.

13. Letter from Anne Brontë to Ellen Nussey, 5th April 1849, ms. Brontë Parsonage Museum.

14. Letter from Charlotte Brontë to Ellen Nussey, 1st May 1849, ms. Pierpont Morgan Library, New York.

15. Nussey, Ellen, *A Short Account of The Last Days of Dear A.B.*, ms. King's School Library, Canterbury.

16. Brontë, Anne, The Penitent.

17. Brontë, Anne, *Agnes Grey*, pp. 145-6.

The Search for Anne Brontë's Last Words

1. Brontë, Charlotte, On The Death of Anne Brontë.
2. Letter from Charlotte Brontë to Ellen Nussey, 23rd December 1848, ms. Berg Collection, New York Public Library.
3. Letter from Thomas Cautley Newby to Emily Brontë, 15th February 1848, ms. Brontë Parsonage Museum.
4. Moore, George, *Conversations in Ebury Street*, p. 220.
5. Brontë, Anne, *The Tenant of Wildfell Hall*, p. 3.
6. Brontë, Charlotte, *Biographical Notice of Ellis and Acton Bell*, ms. British Library, London.
7. Diary paper of Anne Brontë, 30th July 1841, ms. Law collection.

The Message in Anne Brontë's Last Words

1. Brontë, Anne, *The Tenant of Wildfell Hall*, p. 138.
2. Lock, John and Dixon, William Thomas, *A Man of Sorrow: The Life, Letters and Times of the Rev. Patrick Brontë*, p. 369.
3. Brontë, Anne, Self Congratulation, (for the full poem, see the opening of Chapter Four).
4. Thormälen, Marianne, *The Brontës and Religion*, p. 223.
5. Letter from Anne Brontë to Reverend David Thom, 30th December 1848, ms. Princeton University, New Jersey.
6. Brontë, Anne, *The Tenant of Wildfell Hall*, p. 98.
7. Letter from Charlotte Brontë to W. S. Williams, 5th September 1850, ms. Parrish Collection, Princeton University.
8. Brontë, Charlotte, *Biographical Notice of Ellis and Acton Bell*, ms. British Library, London.

1. Matthew Arnold was an influential Victorian poet and critic, aged 28 when he met Charlotte at Fox How in Ambleside – the home of William Wordsworth's son-in-law, Edward Quillinan. He is less than praising of Charlotte's appearance here, and he was also damning of her novels, and yet in 1855, shortly after Charlotte's death, he wrote a beautiful poem in praise of the Brontës entitled 'Haworth Churchyard'.

2. Phrenology is the study of bumps on the forehead, which some believe can reveal an individual's personality and future. It was very popular in the nineteenth century, and Charlotte was a firm believer in it – her friend Mary Taylor wrote of how Charlotte loved to feel and then assess her friends' foreheads. In 1851 her publisher George Smith, knowing Charlotte's interest in the subject, took her to see T. P. Brown on the Strand. He was one of England's leading phrenologists and this is his report which he sent to Smith after examining Charlotte. It should be noted that he did not know who she was or what she did, as Smith had introduced her to him as a 'Miss Fraser'.

3. 'In Memoriam', the great poem by Alfred Tennyson, was written in 1849. Tennyson had been one of the writers sent unsold copies of *Poems by Currer, Ellis and Acton Bell* by Anne and her sisters in 1847.

4. Tartar is Shirley Keeldar's dog in Charlotte Brontë's novel *Shirley*. Just as Shirley was a portrait of Emily, Tartar was a portrait of her dog, Keeper.

5. Devonia was the pen name of an unknown Fraser's Magazine contributor.

6. William Dearden was a Keighley schoolmaster, minor poet and friend of Branwell Brontë. He became one of the fiercest defenders of the Brontë family, and especially

of Patrick Brontë against the inaccuracies in Elizabeth Gaskell's *Life of Charlotte Brontë*. This is one of a number of letters he sent to local papers on the subject; Patrick at one point asked him to desist from writing them, but to no avail.

7. Richard Hengist Horne was a popular poet and dramatist of his day, and Charlotte Brontë was a great fan of his most famous work 'Orion'. He lived a colourful life before devoting himself to literature, spending many years as a mercenary, fighting for Mexican independence.

8. An interesting comment from Charlotte's fellow guest. Did the guests know her father's background, or is this a sign that in adulthood Charlotte retained the noticeably Irish accent that her friend Mary Taylor said she possessed in childhood?

9. Although not published until 1893 the reporter indicates that this interview took place in 1876 or 1877, so we have used this as the basis for its chronological order – thus placing it, correctly, before our second encounter with Nancy which finds her in very altered circumstances.

10. During her time as a Brontë servant, Nancy used the surname Garrs, but in fact her family was French in origin and the surname was de Garrs. She married twice, becoming first Nancy Wainwright and then Nancy Malone.

11. Sir Thomas Wemyss Reid was a nineteenth century Brontë biographer.

12. Parsonage servant Tabby Aykroyd never fully recovered from a badly broken leg in 1836, but the Brontë siblings insisted that she remain at the Parsonage. In 1839 she retired to live with her sister, but in 1842 she returned to Haworth Parsonage where she lived until her death, shortly before Charlotte's, in 1855.

13. Originally Sarah de Garrs (Nancy's younger sister), she married William Newsome and later emigrated to America, living in Ohio and then Iowa.

14. Francis Leyland was a brother of the Halifax sculptor Joseph Leyland, and author of the 1886 biography *The Brontë Family*. He had been a friend of Branwell Brontë, and his book and letters to newspapers were written with the aim of defending Branwell's reputation.

15. Despite being referred to as Nancy Wainwright throughout the article, Nancy was by this time the widowed Nancy Malone.

16. This younger woman could be the Parsonage servant Martha Brown, who became a friend of Charlotte's after Anne's death left her alone, but it is more likely to be her great friend Ellen Nussey, who often visited the Parsonage. Although only a year younger than Charlotte, Ellen had a youthful appearance.

17. These boots must once have belonged to Branwell Brontë, and had been kept after his death.

18. Abraham Holroyd was a bookshop owner and local historian from Thornton, the Bradford birthplace of the Brontës.

19. Brontë, Charlotte, *Jane Eyre*, p. 300.

20. After leaving Haworth, the Horsfall family emigrated to Australia. John Sutcliffe Horsfall became a landowner and wool trader there, becoming very wealthy in the process.

21. Mr Feather is obviously talking here about Patrick Branwell the son, rather than Patrick the father.

22. Perhaps this is because Mrs Hartley's teacher is much more likely to have been Charlotte or Anne Brontë than the reserved Emily?

23. This then is Jane, the daughter of John Greenwood,

the Haworth stationer and friend of the Brontë family.

24. The 1861 census does indeed show a Brontë Green-wood born in 1859 – two years before Patrick's death, but at a time when he was very ill. Further records show that Brontë Greenwood emigrated to America on the SS Rhynland in 1900 where he became a successful barrister. After the opening of the Brontë Parsonage Museum in 1928 he returned to Haworth to visit it, and he later paid for the restoration of Haworth's church.

25. Reverend James Bradley was curate of Oakworth, a neighbouring parish of Haworth. He was known for playing a flute, and Charlotte Brontë portrayed him as the flute playing Reverend David Sweeting in *Shirley*.

26. Reverend Joseph Grant was curate of Oxenhope, another neighbouring parish, and had previously been an assistant curate to Patrick in Haworth. He was a close friend of Arthur Bell Nicholls and acted as his best man. Reverend Sutcliffe Sowden was another friend, and he conducted the wedding ceremony.

27. There was one other person present – Margaret Wooler who signed the marriage record as a witness along-side Ellen Nussey. This former teacher of Anne Brontë also gave Charlotte away, as Patrick said he was too ill to attend the wedding.

28. James Roberts was the son of a Haworth weaver who became a wealthy industrialist and mill owner. He was made a Baronet, and in 1928 he bought Haworth Parson-age when it was put up for sale by the Church of England and gifted it to the Brontë Society to use as a museum.

29. Tabitha Ratcliffe, née Brown, was the youngest daughter of John Brown the Haworth sexton, and sister of the Parsonage servant Martha Brown. On occasion, Tabitha had also helped out at the Parsonage.

Select Bibliography

Alexander, Christine and Sellars, Jane, *The Art of The Brontës*, Cambridge University Press, 1995

Alexander, Christine [ed.], *Tales of Glass Town, Angria, and Gondal*, Oxford World's Classics, 2010

Atkinson, E., *Haworth In The Brontë Era, B.H.Babbage's Visit To Haworth*, Keighley, 1998

Barker, Juliet, *The Brontës*, Weidenfeld & Nicolson, 1994

Barnard, Robert and Louise [ed.], *A Brontë Encyclopedia*, Blackwell, 2007

Chadwick, Ellis H., *In the Footsteps of the Brontës*, Pitman, 1913

Chitham, Edward, *A Life of Anne Brontë*, Blackwell, 1991

Denton, D. M., *Without The Veil Between*, All Things That Matter Press, 2017

Dinsdale, Ann, *The Brontës At Haworth*, Frances Lincoln, 2006

du Maurier, Daphne, *The Infernal World of Branwell Brontë*, Penguin, 1972

Fawkes, Glynis, *Charlotte Brontë Before Jane Eyre*, Disney-Hyperion, 2019

Gaskell, Elizabeth, *The Life of Charlotte Brontë*, Smith, Elder & Co., 1857

Gérin, Winifred, *Anne Brontë*, Allen Lane, 1959

Gérin, Winifred, *Charlotte Brontë*, Oxford University Press, 1967

Gérin, Winifred, *Emily Brontë*, Oxford University Press, 1971

Green, Dudley, *Patrick Brontë: Father of Genius*, The History Press, 2008

Grundy, Francis, *Pictures of The Past*, Griffith & Farrar, 1879

Harland, Marion, *Charlotte Brontë At Home*, Kessinger Publishing, 2010

Harman, Claire, *Charlotte Brontë: A Life*, Viking, 2015

Holland, Nick, *In Search of Anne Brontë*, The History Press, 2016

Ingham, Patricia, *The Brontës*, Oxford University Press, 2008

Langland, Elizabeth, *Anne Brontë: The Other One*, Palgrave Macmillan, 1989

Lemon, Charles [ed.], *Classics of Brontë Scholarship*, The Bronte Society, 1999

Leyland, Francis, *The Brontë Family*, Hurst & Blackett, 1886

Lister, Philip, *Ghosts & Gravestones of Haworth*, Tempus, 2006

MacEwan, Helen, *The Brontës in Brussels*, Peter Owen, 2014

Miller, Lucastra, *The Brontë Myth*, Jonathan Cape, 2001

Moore, George, *Conversations In Ebury Street*, William Heinemann, 1930

Neufeldt, Victor A. [ed.], *The Works of Patrick Branwell Brontë: 1837-1848*, Routledge, 2017

Orel, Harold, *The Brontës: Interviews and Recollections*, Palgrave MacMillan, 1996

Shorter, Clement, *The Brontës and Their Circle*, J.M. Dent, 1914

Smith, George, *A Memoir With Some Pages of Biography*, Cambridge University Press, 2012

Smith, Margaret [ed.], *The Letters of Charlotte Brontë (Volumes 1-3)*, Clarendon Press, 1995

Spark, Muriel, *The Essence of The Brontës*, Peter Owen, 1993

Thormälen, Marianne, *The Brontës and Religion*, Cambridge University Press, 2002

The versions of the books by the Brontë sisters referred to within the notes are as follows:

Brontë, C., E., and A., *Poems by Currer, Ellis, and Acton Bell*, Aylott & Jones, 1846

Brontë, Anne, *Agnes Grey*, Wordsworth Classics, 1998

Brontë, Anne, *The Tenant of Wildfell Hall*, Wordsworth Classics, 1994

Brontë, Charlotte, *Jane Eyre*, Wordsworth Classics, 1999

Brontë, Charlotte, *Shirley*, Collins Classics, 2012

9 781912 436361